Christopher Roßmann

Customer journey analytics for the financial sector

How do customers make decisions regarding their bank?

Bibliografische Information der Deutschen Nationalbibliothek:

Die Deutsche Nationalbibliothek verzeichnet diese Publikation in der Deutschen Nationalbibliografie; detaillierte bibliografische Daten sind im Internet über http://dnb.d-nb.de abrufbar.

Impressum:

Ein Imprint der Open Publishing GmbH, München

Druck und Bindung: Books on Demand GmbH, Norderstedt, Germany

Covergestaltung: Open Publishing GmbH

Abstract

The relevance of traditional advisor-based bank consultations is in decline. Less young people consider the profession of a qualified bank advisor as a professional career perspective and more customers call an online bank their primary financial provider. The financial industry is facing wide-ranging changes due to historically low interest rates, higher regulation and in particular, the rise of online banks and digitization. Traditional retail banks in Germany have been losing market share, bank branches have been merged as well as products and services changed. However, the German savings banks have been pursuing a comprehensive consultation approach (Sparkassen-Finanzkonzept) aiming to build a competitive advantage, increase customer loyalty and expand the product usage rate by existing customers. With a view to customers, the exploration of the decision-making process regarding banks and their financial products and services is pivotal for the bank's strategic process and product management as well as marketing measures. While customer surveys and market analysis are widely spread to adopt strategic implications, an in-depth elaboration of the customer's journey is an almost untouched approach to gain insight into the customers experience. This study conducts a customer journey analysis to examine the experience of actual customers with a focus on comprehensive bank consultations in German savings banks and thereby uncovers reasons for a low perception of the consultation approach by customers. The paper provides improvement proposals for several units of the bank. An improved target vision for the customer journey is developed and contains minor and major possible managerial implications.

Table of Contents

Abbreviations and Acronyms

%	Percent
ATM	Automated teller machine
CEO	Chief executive officer
CES	Customer effort score
CJA	Customer journey analytics
CJM	Customer journey mapping
CLV	Customer lifetime value
COO	Chief operations officer
CR	Conversion rate
CRM	Customer relationship management
etc.	Et cetera / and so on
e.g.	Exempli gratia / for example
Girocard	Debit card
IT	Information technology
KPI	Key performance indicator
MasterCard SecureCode	Online authorization method for credit cards by Mastercard
NPS	Net promoter score
OSP-Neo	One system plus neo
ROI	Return on investment
ROPO	Research online - purchase offline
RR	Retention rate
Sbroker	Sparkassen-Broker: business associate providing securities accounts
SFK	Sparkassen-Finanzkonzept / comprehensive bank consultation concept

TAN	Transaction authentication number
US	United States of America
UX	Customer experience

List of Figures

List of Tables

1 Introduction

The first chapter introduces the thesis and describes author's personal motivation and decision for the chosen topic. Following, the objective and focus of this paper is stated. Finally, the reply structure to the research question is described.

1.1 Professional Background and Motivation

I have been working for a German savings bank[1] for more than 10 years, and in doing so, always pursued a high customer-orientation on my job. At first, in a branch manager position in the retail banking unit. In this position, I consulted customers on financial products and in doing so, applied the comprehensive consultation concept. Currently, I am holding a management position as the head of unit for the sales distribution and marketing department of the bank. My former and current job both significantly affect the experience of customers using products and receiving advice from bank customer advisors. The more professional experience I gained in the financial industry, the more I lost the capability to imagine the customer's experience from their view. As a result, I decided to choose this topic to gain insight into the customer's point of view. Moreover, profound literature and studies about customer journey analytics carried out within a German savings bank are not available and therefore, the research field is interesting. Additionally, customer journey analytics can support to solve actual business issues and improve the customer experience to aim for corporate objectives. This is in the fundamental interest of my professional activities.

1.2 Purpose and Research Questions

The purpose of this study is to explore the experience of private retail bank customers regarding the comprehensive bank consultation approach (Sparkassen-Finanzkonzept, SFK)[2] of the savings banks in Germany. The study aims for solving the business issue *"low perception of the value and benefits of comprehensive bank consultations by private retail bank customers of savings banks in Germany"*. Due to a lack of studies available proofing the actual evidence of the business issue, it is

1 Reference removed due to data protection policy.

2 The aim of this paper is for international accessibility by researchers, and therefore, specialist terms and the underlying concepts of the German retail banking sector and the savings banks in particular, are explained.

considered a hypothesis. The research question is addressed through conducting a customer journey analysis with actual customers, further empirical research and complemented with theoretical findings.[3] The empirical part mainly focuses on the sample bank Sparkasse 1.[4] The study finally provides initial managerial implications to reach an improved target vision of the examined customer journey. Further quantitative and qualitative research is recommended to validate practical implementations proposed in this study.

1.3 Outline of the Thesis

The **second chapter** describes and defines central terms of the research topic based on reviewing relevant literature and studies. The **third chapter** is based on theoretical findings and briefly describes the current developments and challenges of the financial industry and additionally their strategic directions on channels. Thus, it provides required industry-relevant background knowledge for the further paper. Following, considerations for implementing a customer journey analytics project at a financial services provider are elaborated and subsequently, the theoretical customer journey is illustrated. The **fourth chapter** describes and evaluates the applied research design and data collection methods. This groundwork lays the base for the empirical research in **chapter five**, which firstly describes the findings of the conducted empirical research. Secondly, the findings are generally discussed and evaluated. At this point, gained theoretical knowledge is applied to portray empirical results in customer journey maps which are complemented with initial improvement suggestions for the sample bank. Finally, **chapter six** combines and aggregates the empirical findings to create a customer journey map of the target vision. Managerial implications are provided and their feasibility and workload are evaluated. Intended effects on defined indicators in the sample bank are explained. The final **chapter seven** briefly summarizes the key results and critically reflects the recommendations and the research design.

---

3 The theoretical part of this study is derived from academic resources. Due to the practical character of the topic, certain resources -which can be considered as non-academic- were utilized. In that case, the resources were set in an appropriate context.

4 Sparkasse 1 is a German savings bank located in XXX, Germany and part of the German Savings Banks Finance Group. The Bank is independent and locally managed. Its balance sheet total is XXX Euro. The total number of retail checking accounts is XXX. Due to the general corporate strategy of the savings banks, the bank`s business activities are concentrated on customers in the region of Sparkasse 1. [Reference removed due to data protection policy.]

2 Customer Journey Analytics (CJA)

2.1 Introduction and Definition

The purpose of customer journey analytics (CJA) is to help understand the experience a customer makes using a product or service of an organization, also described as "walking in customer's shoes".[5] It provides a structure for the sequence of experiences a customer makes purchasing a product or using a service. Every step a customer makes is described separately.[6] A customer journey is also known as experience journey or user journey, oftentimes displayed on a customer experience map.[7] Research- and business-related applications of the CJA are most commonly published under the term customer journey mapping (CJM). This mapping is described below.

Customer journey analytics is based on the single customer experiences of subordinate journeys, which can last minutes to years.[8] However, most analyses in the field of CJA and mapping are carried out on journeys with durations of minutes or hours. This can be in contrast to customer lifecycle maps, which are clearly distinguishable by their broader approach based on lifetime relationships between a customer and an organization.[9] All the single journeys and touchpoints a customer goes through with an organization and the brand build the foundation for their individual customer lifecycle map.

Segelstroem (2013) states that the most commonly used elements of CJAs are:

- Time-aspects
- Interactions
- Emotional triggers

According to Segelstroem (2013) customer journey maps are appropriate to interpret customer research by service designers.[10]

---

5 cf. Holmlid / Evenson (2008), p. 343

6 cf. Nguyen / Pupillo (2012), pp. 317-330

7 cf. Segelstroem (2013), p. 168

8 cf. Sauro, J. (2015), p. 92

9 cf. Kalbach, J. (2018), p. 256

10 Service design is the activity of improving or creating services with a focus on meeting the user's or customer's needs. [cf. The interaction design foundation (ed.) (2018), retrieved from https://www.interaction-design.org/]

Suppliers have to consider a wide range of factors when it comes to offering products and services such as:

- legal requirements,
- profits and costs,
- efficiency of processes,
- corporate culture,
- competitors,
- and conflicts of interest within the organization.

The success of products and services is most commonly measured utilizing quantitative factors such as the churn rate or sales figures. Customer satisfaction is also measured using quantitative factors found in customer polls and studies by third parties by management consultancies.

CJAs have a different approach and focus exclusively on the customer experience. The customer experience results stem from the interactions between a customer and an organization. This includes both the conscious and unconscious experiences.[11]

CJA or customer journey mapping (CJM) can be considered as part of the broader approach of customer analytics. Most activities of customer analytics are derived from the evaluation of large amounts of data (big data), e.g. customer purchase records, transactional data, or surveys. Further analytical methods utilize statistical analysis to detect patterns in customer behavior.[12] In contrast to these metric-based approaches, CJA, and in particular CJM, focuses on the individual customer level by examining the behaviors and experiences of just a few chosen customers. Oberholzer & Eichholzer (2017) recommend interviewing a total of eight customers for the CJA project.[13] In conclusion, CJAs are compiled by big data as described above and small data[14] to find detailed insights into the customer's behavior. The CJM described and applied in this paper is based on small data only.

[11] cf. SAS Institute Inc. (ed.) (n.d.), retrieved from https://www.sas.com/

[12] cf. Sauro, J. (2015), p. 8

[13] cf. Oberholzer / Eichholzer (2017), p. 21

[14] Small datasets contain typically less than 30 customers [cf. Sauro, J. (2015), p. 12].

2.2 Customer Journey Mapping (CJM)

The experiences of an individual customer are illustrated in customer journey maps. These maps cover the decision-making process and other choices a customer makes, e.g. opening a bank account or staying a loyal customer.[15] The purpose is to understand and address customer needs and pain points.[16] The map combines the storytelling of the customer's experiences and its visualization, which helps to identify problem areas during the different stages a customer goes through: (1) becoming aware of the product or service, (2) purchasing it, and then finally (3) using it. Additionally, it helps determine opportunities to improve a product, service or process within an organization. This also includes contradictory processes and actions within the same organization. While different departments organize their actions based on a defined operational and organizational structure, they can indeed compete with each other without even being aware of it. CJM can provide insight into these unfavorable conditions by illustrating the customer's entire experience on a comprehensive map.[17,18] The customer acts as a process evaluator and development manager.

Overall, the key elements of CJM suitable for different industries can be categorized in three main groupings:[19,20,21]

1. **Customer's viewpoint:** this category is the most important part of the CJM and describes the actions and feelings of the customer. It includes **pain and pleasure points**. While pain points describe actual or perceived negative experiences, pleasure points describe the opposite, i.e. positive experiences. In this paper, pain points are defined as any experience a customer has, where the organization does not meet their expectations. Pleasure points are defined as experiences, which surpass the customer's expectations of a product or service.

The customer viewpoint can be distinguished also into three parts:[22]

15 cf. Kalbach, J. (2018), p. 6
16 cf. Kaplan (2016), retrieved from https://www.nngroup.com/
17 cf. Sauro, J. (2015), p. 87
18 see also chapter 3.3.1 for a definition of silo mentality.
19 cf. Kalbach, J. (2018), pp. 6-9
20 cf. Kaplan (2016), retrieved from https://www.nngroup.com/
21 cf. Custer, L. (2018), retrieved from http://asq.org/
22 cf. Oberholzer / Eichholzer (2017), pp. 3-6

a. Actions and comments

All steps, actions, and comments the customer makes on their journey are documented neutrally in regard to touchpoints.

b. Perceptions

Basically everything that one could conceive as a customer perception is recoded. These are mainly defined as functions, services and noises. This also includes the behavior of any persons, e.g. employees and other customers.

c. Emotions

Pain and pleasure points and emotions are considered here. Emotions are described on a curve and can be positive, neutral, or negative. Their intensity varies.

2. **Interactions of customer with organization:** this category is the connection from the customer to the organization and vice versa. There are several ways to connect through a wide variety of channels. Every single case of "touching" the organization by the customer counts. These touchpoints are described below.

3. **Organization's viewpoint:** the organization implements process and activities to generate touchpoints. Additionally, strengths and weaknesses of each step in the customer journey are identified. Additionally, chances and risks are determined. This category is the first step in the process to improve products and services, which result from CJA projects.

2.3 Touchpoints

There are different approaches to define and cluster touchpoints. Touchpoints are defined as the interactions between a customer and an organization.[23,24] They are often considered as the channels of an organization and listed by the organization's departments. However, this view is criticized as too company-focused and isolates departments into silos. Channels are clustered in general categories from the company's point of view, while touchpoints are described more specifically from the customer's point of view.[25] For instance: a call center is considered a channel, which covers inbound and outbound phone calls for scheduling appointments with a customer advisor. Inbound and outbound phone calls are two separate touchpoints. The call center is one single channel. Both touchpoints are based on using a

23 cf. Oberholzer / Eichholzer (2017), p. 5

24 cf. Maechler / Neher / Park (2016), retrieved from https://www.mckinsey.com/

25 cf. Walters (n.d.), retrieved from http://360connext.com/

singular channel for the same purpose; the touchpoints are different: an inbound phone call requires an activity originated by the customer, while outbound phone calls to acquire appointments have a totally different character. The same applies to third-company touchpoints like reviews of the organization. The website of an organization is also considered a channel. Checking customer reviews on Google is a touchpoint. In contrast, once the customer gets directed to the company's official website, he starts using a channel.

This can be related to the traditional funnel approach of touchpoints. In this approach, marketing is a one-way street: all marketing is directed to the customer. The customer decides which product he picks at the end of a funnel – after considering other brands. There are several different types of marketing funnels available, but they are all based on the same traditional principle: a non-dynamic funnel.[26] This approach lacks the consideration of the customer's point of view and their interactions with the company, e.g. writing a review. Today's marketing and customer's decision-making process is more dynamic due to more competititors and choices as well as digitization. The consumer decision journey tries to incorporate the decision-making process of customers in the current environment.[27]

26 cf. Sauro, J. (2015), pp. 88-89 for an overview of the most commonly used approaches: Forrester Funnel, Diffusion of Innovation, Principles of Marketing

27 cf. Court, Elzinga, Mulder, Vetvik (2009), retrieved from https://www.mckinsey.com/

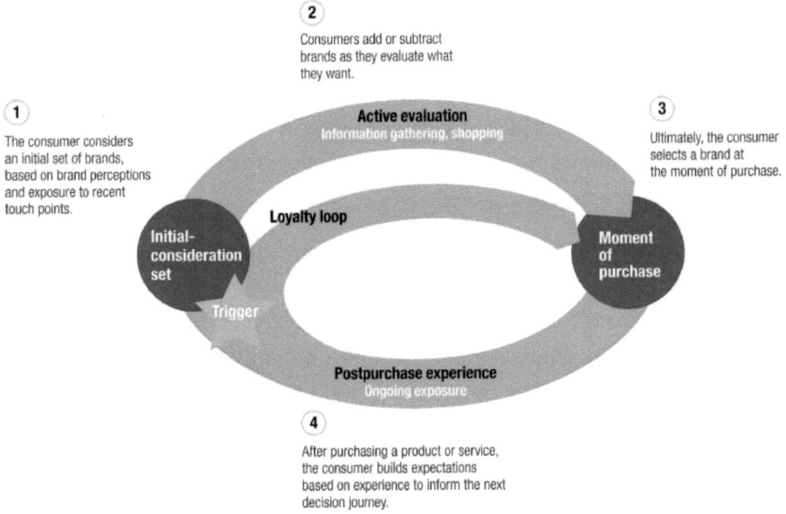

Figure 1: The consumer decision journey by McKinsey28

Oberholzer and Eichholzer (2017) describe the customer experience circle to capture the entire relationship between a customer and the organization. The circle is illustrated on the next page.

28 Source: Court, Elzinga, Mulder, Vetvik (2009), retrieved from https://www.mckinsey.com/

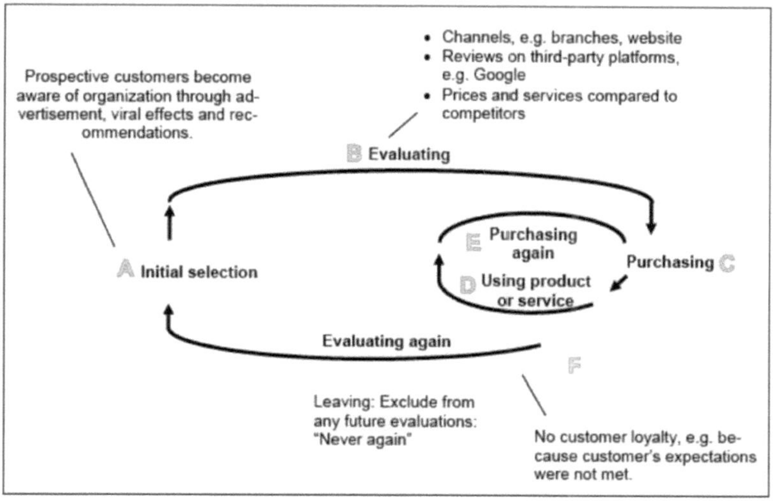

Figure 2: The customer journey in the customer experience cycle29

Business problems can occur anywhere along the journey and within the different stages of the customer experience circle. The examination of business problems for deriving solutions as well as management implications are key goals of a CJA project.

Examples for the customer experience cycle (figure 2):

A) Why are our products and services less exciting and lead to lower viral effects compared to our competitors?

B) Why do our customer advisors schedule more consultations than other competitors, but are less successful in actually selling the products?

C) How can we increase the rate of existing customers purchasing additional supplementary or complementary products or packages?

D) Why do customers complain frequently about technical issues of our products?

E) How can we increase customer loyalty?

F) Why has the termination rate increased recently?

---

29 adapted from Oberholzer / Eichholzer (2017), p. 14

3 Customer Journey Analytics in the Financial Industry

3.1 The Financial Industry in the Current Environment

Germany has a three-tiered banking system made up of private banks, public savings banks and cooperative banking associations. The development of this unique system has a long history and leads to the highest relation of banks per capita of all developed countries. This results in an excess capacity of branches and bank employees.[30] Online banks with a limited number of products and services operate without a cost-intensive network of branches and customer advisors. They have become increasingly important during the last two decades. While the customer numbers totaled only 3.9 million in the year 2000, the expectation for the year 2020 is upwards of 22 million customers.[31] Compared to other countries, German customers are more likely to use an online bank as their primary financial institution. A survey from 2016 revealed that only 74% of customers in the German market consider a traditional financial institution with branches as their primary financial institution;[32] the same survey showed higher results (81%) in the US market.[33] Online banks are the most successful market player in gaining market share in Germany. They are considered as primary financial institution by 20 % of customers in Germany, compared to an average 10 % in other countries.[34]

Online Banks pursue the simple strategic approach of offering certain products with less service and for lower or no fees. Traditional financial institutions in Germany have been responding by implementing or improving a comprehensive conceptual product, service, and consultation approach with a large product portfolio to cover all needs and wants of their customers. While the fact that online banks have simply gained more customers is a clear issue for the traditional institutions, a large number of Germans consider an online bank as their primary financial institution, which is a far more serious than a simple warning signal. This indicates that the traditional institutions' approach of the comprehensive consultation

---

30 cf. Cermak, C. (2017), retrieved from https://global.handelsblatt.com/

31 cf. Investors Marketing Management Consultants (ed.) (2016), retrieved from http://www.investors-marketing.de/

32 cf. Ernst & Young (ed.) (2016), retrieved from https://www.ey.com/

33 cf. Ernst & Young (ed.) (2016b), retrieved from https://www.ey.com/

34 cf. Ernst & Young (ed.) (2016), retrieved from https://www.ey.com/

concept is either not wanted by a significant number of customers or its benefits are not perceived valuable by them. Moreover, online banks are more profitable than their traditional counterparts.[35] Customer relationship management systems (CRM) have become more common recently. These IT solutions aim for managing customer relationships and increase revenues by collecting and analyzing data of customer behavior.[36]

The German banking sector appears to be especially overbanked. The average return on equity of the German banking sector indicates just that. Between 2004 and 2015, the average return on equity was a meager 2%. Comparing the German market to banks in France (8%), the UK (6%), Japan (4%), Switzerland (7%) and the US (8%), the assumption that German banks have far-reaching changes ahead is obvious.[37] With this in mind, the personnel base working in the sector has been stable since 2007 and it is the third largest employment sector with a share of 1.3% of the total labor force after the mechanical construction (2.3%) and the automotive sector (1.8%).[38]

The occurrence of Fintech is the most recent threat for traditional German financial institutions. These start-ups combine technology and financial services to create an innovative benefit for customers.[39] The customer potential of Fintech is estimated at 40% of internet users or 31 % of the population in Germany.[40] Ernst & Young came to similar results in their own study from 2017, stating that 35% of the population are prospective Fintech adopters.[41] The march of technology has forced traditional institutions to find innovative solutions to this development that endangers the checking account as the most important base product. Losing transactions to Fintech, non-banks and near-banks are putting additional pressure on customers, affecting their loyalty to traditional banking institutions leading to decreasing revenues. In a representative survey, 22% of respondents state that they would consider financial products from Amazon, Facebook, Google, or Apple;

---

35 cf. The Economist (ed.) (2017), retrieved from https://www.economist.com/

36 cf. Plettenberg, P. / Kaucic, A. (2016), retrieved from https://www.atkearney.it/

37 cf. Cermak, C. (2017), retrieved from https://global.handelsblatt.com/

38 cf. Koch / Floetotto / Weigl / Schrock (2016), retrieved from https://www.mckinsey.com/

39 cf. Dorfleitner / Hornuf (2016), p. 1

40 cf. Olmann, M. / Pramann, J.-A. (2016), p. 96

41 cf. Ernst & Young (ed.) (2017), retrieved from http://www.ey.com/

almost 14% would consider opening a checking account with the mentioned providers acting as non-/near-banks.[42]

Germany's banks have been slow in developing and forcing digitization.[43] For instance, contactless payments have a high growth rate, but only have a share of 1% compared to 47.6% of cash payments in Germany.[44] This statistic is one of several indicators to judge the level of implementation of new technologies in the sector.

Finally, the banking sector is challenged by historically low interest rates and regulations that have been resulting in branch closures[45], merges of institutions, and the rise of selling third-party commission-based products. Due to these reasons, advising customers has become more important as it enhances the opportunity to up-sell and cross-sell additional products to earn revenues independent of the market interest rates and equities.

In conclusion, the retail banking sector in Germany is facing the following current challenges and developments:

- Online banks are relatively popular. Their market share is still growing.
- Traditional financial institutions have a large network of branches. This is a major reason why the sector is the least profitable in regard to other developed countries.
- New innovative competitors and changing customer demands for digital solutions make it necessary to catchup with the digital development.
- Historically low interest rates enhance opportunities to sell commission-based third-party products.
- A stable, large labor force remains as it has in the past.

The developments and changes listed above are directly impacting the customer journey in banking. There are further developments challenging traditional banks, which affect the customer journey to a lesser extent and are not included in the scope of this paper. Those not included in the scope are briefly described below:[46]

---

42 cf. Soldwedel, A. / Inhoffen, L. (2018), retrieved from https://yougov.de/

43 cf. GFT Technologies (ed.) (2017), p. 9

44 cf. Deutsche Bundesbank (ed.) (2017), p. 24

45 cf. Schwarz / Dapp / Beck / Khussainova (2017), retrieved from https://www.kfw.de/

46 cf. Henk, A. / Holthaus, J.-U. (2015), pp. 63-64

- Globalization with an increased international competition in the supply and value chain.
- Demographic changes with an aging society and migration to urban areas.
- More corporate responsibility and sustainability reporting requirements with regard to climate change and ethical criteria.
- More banking regulations and supervision.

3.2 Channel Strategy

In this chapter, the most important currently applied distribution and marketing channels of the German retail banking sector are listed and described briefly. Then, changes in the strategies of the sector are predicted.

Most important sales and marketing channels of the German savings banks and the private banking sector are:[47,48]:

- Branch
  - Customer advisor and service employees
  - Paper-based and digital advertisement (e.g. on ATM screens)
- Online banking
- Mobile banking app
- Website
- Social media
- Inbound and outbound calls

In a study carried out by Horváth & Partners Management Consultants (2015), approximately 100 employees in management positions at banks and insurance providers were consulted regarding the multi-channel strategic approach of banks and insurances in Germany. Nearly 61% of them agreed on the hypothesis: *"customer advisors consult and care of their customers exclusively on the single sales channel on which the product was initially sold."*[49]

According to this study, the integration of different sales and marketing channels to create a coherent customer experience is not applied in a satisfactory manner.

47 cf. Sparkassen- und Giroverband Hessen-Thüringen (ed.) (2018), pp. 14-15

48 cf. Deloitte Development LLC (ed.) (2017), retrieved from https://www2.deloitte.com/

49 cf. Horváth & Partners Management Consultants (ed.) (2015), p. 6

The consumer journey is highly influenced by the distribution strategy and how different channels interact with each other. In particular, the German banking sector was subject to wide-ranging changes in customer channel demands.

The target vision of the multi-channel approach aims for a coherent multi-channel strategy. The different marketing and sales channels are integrated to avoid competing with each other or being considered separately. In this approach, the customer advisor has an overall responsibility for the customer and does not care about which channel the customer chooses.[50] This offers interesting insights and conclusions for the customer journey. Indeed, the internal and external view of a journey can differ significantly.

As mentioned earlier, some activities of different departments of an organization can contradict each other. According to the conclusions from Horváth & Partners Management Consultants (2015) different channels actually compete with each other in the financial industry. This can be traced back to the widespread application of sales goals for customer advisors over certain sales channels. As the study suggests, sales goals for customer advisors should be measured independently of the channels the customer uses and not be limited to specific channels.

While Horváth & Partners Management Consultants (2015) still define the target image as a multichannel approach, the term "omnichannel approach" suits better as it explains the current strategic channel approach many traditional banks in Germany take. The mentioned adoptions in the bullet point list are already applied or intended to be applied by those. The major difference between the replaced multichannel approach and its successor is the focus on transactions with a bank-centric view (multichannel) and the focus on interactions with a client-centric view (omnichannel).[51] In other words, completely integrated and synchronized channels are necessary to reach a positive and smooth customer experience without losing information. Customers do not tend to distinguish sales channels and demand a customer journey without friction.[52]

---

[50] cf. Horváth & Partners Management Consultants (ed.) (2015), pp. 10-11

[51] cf. International Business Machines Corporation (ed.) (n.d.), retrieved from https://www.ibm.com/

[52] cf. Henk, A. / Holthaus, J.-U. (2015), pp. 70-71

Multichannel	Omnichannel
Focused on transactions	Focused on interactions and relationships
Bank-centric view	Customer-centric view
Channels are acting independently and may substitute each other.	Channels are integrated and complement each other.
Products, services, price, and quality differ depending on the channel used.	Coherent perception of the bank and their products for the customer.
Customer experience differs depending on the chosen channel.	Consistent and seamless customer experience across channels.
Customer journey is evaluated and monitored on behalf of separate channels.	Customer journey is evaluated and monitored as a whole.
Disadvantages: customers can not clearly distinguish different channels because brand and distribution strategy are not clearly delineated.	Disadvantages: customers cannot get influenced to use certain channels. A price differentiation based on actual expenses is not applied.

Table 1: Key differences banking-related multichannel and omnichannel approach[53,54,55,56]

An examination of US and Canadian banks published in 2017 states that there is a positive correlation between the channels used and products held by customers. Therefore, customers using multiple channels are more than two times as profitable as those who interact solely through a single channel.[57]

---

53 cf. Weiß, M. (2018), retrieved from https://www.bankenundpartner.de/

54 cf. International Business Machines Corporation (ed.) (n.d.), retrieved from https://www.ibm.com/

55 cf. Levey, Y. (2014), retrieved from https://www.slideshare.net/

56 cf. McKinsey & Company (ed.) (2017), retrieved from https://www.mckinsey.com/

57 cf. McKinsey & Company (ed.) (2017), retrieved from https://www.mckinsey.com/

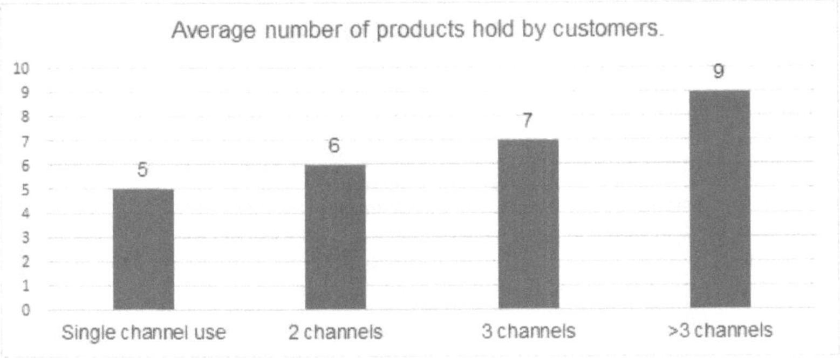

Figure 3: Correlation: channels used and products hold[58]

Another interesting outcome is the implication that customer advisors' sales skills are valuable for the bank. Customers complete purchases with personal consultations in a branch with a 25% higher probability than those completing purchases on digital channels.[59]

A study by McKinsey & Company (2017) supports these findings and reveals a connection between the intensity of communication with the bank and product usage. Credit card customers use their card more often when they interact with the bank through different channels. The level of product usage declines along with the number of channels used by the customer.[60]

The German Savings Banks Association states in a strategy paper that customers visit the branch only once a year, while they get in contact 350 times on digital channels, e.g. website or mobile app. Consultations on complex financial products are still mainly handled by personal consultations in a branch, while basic services like transactions are favorably demanded and offered on digital channels. The strategic approach of the Savings Banks Finance Group states that the consultation of complex financial products is offered in professional consultations in branches due to a lack of customer demand of complex products on other channels.[61]

---

58 adapted from McKinsey & Company (ed.) (2017), retrieved from https://www.mckinsey.com/

59 cf. McKinsey & Company (ed.) (2017), retrieved from https://www.mckinsey.com/

60 cf. McKinsey & Company (ed.) (2017), retrieved from https://www.mckinsey.com/

61 cf. Deutscher Sparkassen- und Giroverband (ed.) (2018), retrieved from https://www.dsgv.de/

Taking a critical look at the multichannel approach and the development of the financial industry in Germany the importance of offering products through multiple channels seems overrated; the advisor-based product sales approach is still the most important due to highly established sales structures in the financial industry in Germany. The demand for financial products is mainly triggered by an integrative marketing and sales strategy with intensive customer handling. The correlation of channels used and products held stated in the study cited above does not proof a causal association. The correlation can also be explained by a higher customer loyalty caused indirectly by intensive communication and channel use. The omnichannel approach is capable of taking into account the necessity of personal consultations supplemented by digital technologies and channels to improve customer experience.

3.3 Implementing a CJA Project at a Financial services provider

3.3.1 Project assignment and consequences

A CJA project can result in improvement proposals with a sizable influence on several units of an organization as stated in Chapter 2.2. The analysis can uncover silo mentality. This attitude occurs in organizations with a lack of capability or willingness of independent divisions to share information freely. The intensity and the consequences on the company's efficiency depend highly on the corporate culture, e.g. the degree of competition as well as process alignment.[62,63] In other words, the customer's journey experiences can be affected negatively through organizational silos.[64]

Therefore, establishing a customer-experience improvement project based on a CJA should be prioritized by the top management.[65] In other words, expecting the analysis to simply validate the process efficiency and customer orientation in the current state will most likely result in inconclusive results[66] as well as wastes time and resources. Indeed, a global examination of CJM reveals that these projects have

---

62 cf. Investopedia (ed.) (n.d.), retrieved from https://www.investopedia.com/

63 cf. Gleeson, B. (2017), retrieved from https://www.forbes.com/

64 for an example cf. Gingiss, D. (2018), retrieved from https://www.forbes.com/

65 cf. Catlin, T. / Duncan, E. / Fanderl, H. / Lorenz, J.-T. (2017), pp. 27-28

66 cf. Wacker, S. (2018), retrieved from https://www.der-bank-blog.de/

the most positive impact on the organization's customer experience, when it is owned by a CEO, COO, or multiple stakeholders.[67]

Depending on the purpose of the analysis and its objectives, the management should take into consideration that CJAs can result in far-reaching implications. Consequently, management should express the willingness to implement strategic, processual, and operational adaptions concluded by the researched journeys. In cases of conducting the CJA for a financial services provider, the sales distribution, marketing, and organization and process management units should be involved in the first step.

3.3.2 Specific CJA characteristics of the financial industry

The prerequisites of a CJA project for financial services providers in a developed country differ significantly from a CJA for simple, one-off purchases, e.g. a TV or new shoes. One key difference is the recognition of the need or want to purchase the item or service by the customer. When the customer recognizes the need or want to purchase a new TV, he actively seeks information and offers online and in retail stores. Of course, former touchpoints with TV brands play a major role for their research.

- In case of financial services, the customer rarely demands for products without the aid of an outside influence. The financial services industry in Germany is highly established given its large number of sales representatives and banks, who active selling these products and services as stated in above. In other words, customers generally only recognize of their need or want with the active involvement of bank advisors.
- Furthermore, the strategic direction to establish lifetime customer loyalty and the specific characteristics in the product design of financial products have to be considered in the initial setup of an CJA project in the financial industry. For example, opening a checking account or applying for a credit card is – from a narrow point of view – a single journey. On the other hand, a credit card is often linked directly to an existing checking account. Applying for and using a credit card is an ongoing journey with several touchpoints and sub-ordinated journeys and services. These touchpoints can be considered separately and independently. However, observations of stand-

67 cf. Mycustomer / Quadient (eds.) (2018), retrieved from https://www.quadient.com/

alone journeys are examined and described in this paper if they are related to the comprehensive consultation approach and can help to improve it.

- Every product hold by the customer determines the overall brand awareness of the customer and directly influences the possibility to expand product usage and to sell additional products. In addition, charges and fees are often paid periodically. The active use of a financial product by the customer is in the interest of a provider as it considerably influences the costs and earnings of the product. Customer analytics play a major role in the industry: non-usage of credit cards or bank accounts increase the possibility of customers cancelling their account. Unusual purchases are indicators of unauthorized transactions (fraud prevention).[68]

For these reasons, the customer journey maps in this paper was complemented with a "Follow-up" and "Long-term" part.[69] In a more stringent interpretation, a customer lifecycle map[70] matches the specific requirements of the financial industry better. To distinguish between the customer lifecycle, a customer journey, and service blueprint is difficult as their approaches overlap in application. Convincing a customer to schedule an appointment for a comprehensive consultation can be considered as a purchase decision in a broader interpretation. As a result, the term customer journey analytics fits the research objective of this paper.

The customer journey maps in this paper are distinguished as four major parts:

1. Pre-consultation

This part describes the awareness of the bank, brand, advisor, product and product usage as well as all activities which are related to the scheduling and start of the appointment.

2. Consultation

The actual consultation is conducted.

68 cf. Sauro, J. (2015), p. 11

69 A follow-up and long-term sequence are also applied in a slightly different context in the samples of customer journey maps in Kalbach, J. (2018), pp. 268-269

70 cf. Bodine, K. (2018), retrieved from https://kerrybodine.com/

3. **Follow-up**

All interactions and touchpoints which come after consultations.

4. **Long-term**

Occurrences not specifically associated to the consultation as well as helpful additional experiences the customer shared.

Due to the myriad of information sources available on the internet and the increase in the number of internet-enabled devices, the customer journey in the financial industry becomes increasingly extensive and confusing. On average, a customer has 11 online touchpoints before completing a bank product. First, it puts the advisor-based consultation approach under pressure. It can lead to a smart and well-prepared customer who is well informed. For instance, in 88% of all processed mortgage loans the customer conducted research online before finally taking out a loan, but only 12% of all processed mortgage loans are processed completely online. Compared to checking account, an online completion without a customer advisor takes place in 47% of the cases. This supports the assumption of the German Savings Banks Association's strategy that complex products require personal consultation.[71] Secondly, tracking the customer journey is becoming more difficult because customers tend to break off their journey through switching channels and media. This places enormous demands on customized advertising activities.[72]

3.3.3 Measuring CJA project success in the financial industry

A CJA project addresses a certain business issue that an organization faces. Once a business issue is identified, key performance indicators (KPI) are set. These indicators measure the success and value created by the applied improvement proposals out of a CJA. KPIs should be separately defined for customers' and organization's perspectives.[73] A more detailed approach clusters the perspectives into four categories: finance, customer, internal process, and education and growth. Finally, a balance scorecard collects the KPIs to help identify internal factors which

---

71 see chapter 3.2

72 cf. GfK Crossmedia Link (ed.) (2017), retrieved from https://www.thinkwithgoogle.com/

73 cf. Oberholzer / Eichholzer (2017), p. 15

influence external results.[74] Furthermore, CJA also identifies issues which were not known when the project was implemented and the journey fragmented.[75]

Selected relevant KPIs for the financial industry and the business issue examined in this paper are:[76,77]

- **Net promoter score (NPS):** the NPS is an indicator for the probability of customers recommending products and services to their contacts.[78] The measure is commonly scale-based and gathered through surveys.[79,80] Customers can be divided into different categories depending on their likelihood to recommend the organization and its products: [81,82]
    - Detractors: those not in favor of the brand and offers and who might damage the reputation through negative reviews.
    - Promoters: those using several products and services and who share good experiences with friends and colleagues.
    - Passive: those called "in-betweens" as they are generally neutral.

A similar approach which also clusters customers of banks in their level of satisfaction and emotional attachment to the organization is applied by the management consultancy Forum Marketing- und Kommunikationsberatung GmbH.[83] The consultancy clusters customers into five categories based on customer satisfaction, likelihood of recommendation, and other attributes. In other words, the level of admiration (fan) is classified:[84]

- Fans: highly satisfied and reliable follower and influencer.
- Sympathizers: satisfied and a follower, but less active in announcing it.

---

74 cf. Kazmierczak, F. / Jelinski (n.d.) (b), retrieved from https://campaign.piwik.pro/

75 cf. Sauro, J. (2015), p. 100

76 cf. Kazmierczak, F. / Jelinski, J. (n.d.), retrieved from https://campaign.piwik.pro/

77 cf. Glenn, R. (n.d.), retrieved from: https://www.digitalagent.com/

78 cf. Sauro, J. (2015), p. 58

79 cf. Oberholzer/Eichholzer (2017), p. 16

80 cf. Sauro, J. (2015), p. 58

81 cf. Sauro, J. (2015), p. 59

82 cf. Glenn, R. (n.d.), retrieved from: https://www.digitalagent.com/

83 cf. Becker, R. / Neitzke, G. (2016), pp. 30-33

84 cf. Forum Marketing und Kommunikationsberatung GmbH (ed.) (n.d.), retrieved from https://forum-mainz.de/

- Mercenaries: satisfied, but price-oriented and less attached.
- Prisoners: dissatisfied due to a lack of information or service, but emotionally attached.
- Enemies: dissatisfied and not attached, tend to complain publicly.

The NPS can be considered as an important indicator for German banks. While for local banks the word-of-mouth recommendations and a positive public reputation matter, for online banks the viral effects and public reviews are pivotal. The empirical part of this study assumes that pleasure points, and in particular any positively surprising experiences the customer makes, improve the NPS.

- **Conversion rate (CR):** an indicator of how many leads are converted into customers. For example: a savings bank offers credit cards on their website and pushes the offer by paid advertisement on social media. The more users who click on the ad on social media and actually purchase a credit card, the higher the conversion rate. A related indicator is the sales qualified leads (SQL) indicator which measures the number of prospective customers converted into actual customers. For instance, how many conducted consultations result in a product completion.
- **Customer lifetime value (CLV):** the CLV indicates the value the customer will bring the organization in the entire business relationship or lifetime[85,86] This factor is pivotal in the banking industry due to the long product lifecycle of financial products and the strategic approach of comprehensive consultations aiming to grow revenue by selling additional products to existing customers (increasing product usage rate per customer).[87] With regard to CJA, the examination of reasons on the different stages of the customer journey which lead to high churn rates is central. The churn rate is the percentage of customers who terminate a contract or stop subscribing to a service.[88]
- **Customer effort score (CES):** the CES measures the friction of the customer's journey and therefore affects the customer acquisition rate and churn rate.[89] It can help to predict customer loyalty and to examine process

85 cf. Cavallone, M. (2017), p. 72 cited from Groenroos, C. (2012), pp. 1520-1534
86 cf. Sauro, J. (2015), pp. 75-76
87 see also chapter 3.1
88 cf. Alawad, N. / Ragheb, M. / Tantawi, P. (2018), pp. 25 & 32
89 cf. Glenn, R. (n.d.), retrieved from: https://www.digitalagent.com/

quality. Customers who describe their experience using their credit cards or checking accounts as easy or effortless are more likely to be loyal customers and do further business with the bank.[90] Additionally, a frictionless channel experience has become more important recently as discussed in Chapter 3.2.

- **Experience rate (UX):** the UX is also called user experience. It measures the customer satisfaction in regard to the immediate use of a product or service. For example, what percent of customers calling the call center or visiting the bank branch to solve an issue would respond in stating that their problem was solved.
- **Retention rate (RR):** percentage of customers who repurchase a product. This indicator is a part in calculating the CLV.[91] It can also be considered independently for a CJA project. For instance, how many customers who applied for a loan, respond to mail offering to extend additional credit. The mailing could be sent six to twelve months after the original loan was paid out.
- There are also other common KPIs to measure the success of a CJA project. However, these are not within the scope of this paper because they are not significantly influential to the business issue and improvement proposals discussed. These less significant KPIs are (selection): return on investment (ROI), active app users, goal canceling rate, engagement metrics and costs per customer acquisition.[92]

3.4 Hypothetical Customer Journey

The German Savings Banks Finance Group has implemented a comprehensive consultation approach called "Sparkassen-Finanzkonzept" building the basis for distinguishing the brand "Sparkasse" and its products and services from its competitors, e.g. online banks. The approach is also called a "Finanzcheck" and builds a structured concept aiming for a standardized sequence for consultations. The concept is simultaneously named Sparkassen-Finanzkonzept (SFK) or comprehensive bank consultation in this paper.

90 cf. Strudley, C. (2015), retrieved from: https://futurethinking.com/
91 cf. Sauro, J. (2015), p. 81
92 cf. Kazmierczak, F. / Jelinski, J. (n.d.), retrieved from https://campaign.piwik.pro/

Furthermore, this approach's objective is to force advisors to sell additional third-party products and collect information from customers to address them with customized offers. This strategic positioning can be considered as a differentiation strategy as it offers higher consultation quality. The comprehensive consultation concept itself is considered a comparative advantage by the savings banks.[93]

The application of a comprehensive consultation approach is an integral part of the strategic direction of the Savings Banks in Germany. For example, it is mentioned first in the chapter 'sales and distribution strategy' in the annual management report of Sparkasse 1,[94] making it a fundamental part of all sales and marketing activities.

With this in mind, the examination of consultations conducted in which the concept was applied is an interesting research object in the current environment of the German savings banks. The CJA in this paper aims to improve the application of the concept and indicate necessary adaptations.

The comprehensive consultation concept is implemented with a guideline for the customer advisors, whereby detailed recommendations are provided for each step of the consultation sequence. The guideline also includes selling points and wording proposals for scheduling appointments and the actual consultation itself. It is offered by the Sparkassenverlag – the central media, advertising, and communication provider of the German Savings Banks Finance Group. The decision to implement the guideline within the sales units, monitoring its application, and quality of the consultations is independently made by every single savings bank.

The following table includes the major steps for the retail banking sector consolidated from the official guidelines[95] and complemented with touchpoints (in particular channels), examples, and an additional following-up step.

---

93 cf. Sparkassen- und Giroverband Hessen-Thueringen (ed.) (2018), pp. 52-54

94 Reference removed due to policies on data protection.

95 cf. Sparkassenverlag (ed.) (2013)

Steps	Details	Touch-points
	Pre-consultation	
Selection of customer	Unit sales distribution selects potential customers for a sales campaign or a customer advisor makes a selection on his own initiative. Either way, socio-economic factors (e.g. age, income) and current product usage are primary selection criteria.	-/-
Preparation	Customer advisor determines reasons for a consultation on the basis of previous consultations and product usage. Customer needs are identified as good as possible. Goal: arouse the customer's interest to schedule an appointment for a consultation.	-/-
Scheduling appointment	Customer advisor calls customer to schedule an appointment for a comprehensive bank consultation. To arouse customer's interest, the advisor emphasizes the value of the consultation and mentions several reasons. Once the customer has agreed, two different dates and times are offered and the estimated duration of the appointment is stated. A binding date is then scheduled.	Phone Customer advisor
	Consultation	
Arriving at branch	Customer arrives at the branch and tells an employee that they have a scheduled appointment with an advisor. (Customer advisors can alternatively schedule the appointment at the customer's home.)	Branch Advertising Service employee Other customers
Waiting	Customer waits in the waiting area to be welcomed by their personal advisor.	See preceding
Welcome	Advisor approaches and welcomes customer and leads them to a separate room where the advisor offers water or coffee. Advisor talks with the customer to build rapport and become more familiar with their needs.	Customer advisor
Procedure is explained / Personal data update	Duration and structure of the consultation is explained. Media of Sparkassen-Finanzkonzept is used to illustrate the comprehensive consultation concept. The personal data of the customer is updated (e.g. employer, address, contact details).	Customer advisor Media[96]

[96] There are several marketing materials (media) offered by Sparkassenverlag to support the consultations by illustrating the structure of the comprehensive consultation concept (Sparkassen-Finanzkonzept).

Steps	**Details**	**Touch-points**
Plans and goals	Customer's future plans regarding the purchase of real estate, other investments, and life goals are identified and listed visibly and transparently.	See preceding.
Current product usage	The concept provides four different parts for the classification of financial products and services used by the customer (competitor products included).[97] Liquidity and services (e.g. checking account) Insurances Retirement provisions Investments and savings Plans, goals, and current product usage are summarized by the advisor to prevent misunderstandings.	See preceding.
Recommendations	Based on the information collected in the previous two steps, the advisor may recommend changing an already existing product in the customer's portfolio or to add an additional product or service. The recommendations provided are standardized based on age and family status. Selling points are based on key attributes of the product solving an issue or satisfying a need the customer mentioned earlier.	Customer advisor Media Printed offer Digital offer Calculations Terms and conditions
Decision	Customer decides if they agree on one or several of the offers.	See preceding.
Contract agreement	Advisor creates paper-based or digital contracts and requests a signature by the customer. Customer reads and checks contracts before signing. Copies of contracts, calculations, offers, and terms and conditions are provided in a folder.	Customer advisor Contract Terms and conditions
Evaluation and completion	Advisor emphasizes main benefits and requests feedback by the customer. Customer is asked to recommend the bank to his relatives and friends.	Customer advisor Media Business cards

97 see also: figure 4

Steps	Details	Touch-points
Follow-up		
Documentation	Notes which were not saved in the digital customer file during the consultation are then saved afterwards by the customer advisor.	-/-
Confirmation	Confirmation of the contract is sent to the customer by mail or a digital copy is uploaded in the online banking mail box.	Mail Website Online banking Mobile app
Monitoring success	The success of consultations is controlled by a central unit (e.g. sales distribution) by measuring key figures consultations per advisor and product sales per consultation.	-/-
Long-term outcome		
Information	The collected information is beneficial for the customer advisor to create prospective individual offers.	Customer advisor Consultations
Information	The collected information enables segmentation criteria (data analytics) for central mailings and other customized advertisement as well as sales campaigns for the sales units (customer advisors).	Mail Online banking Mobile app Call center outbound

Table 2: The consultation sequence of the comprehensive consultation concept

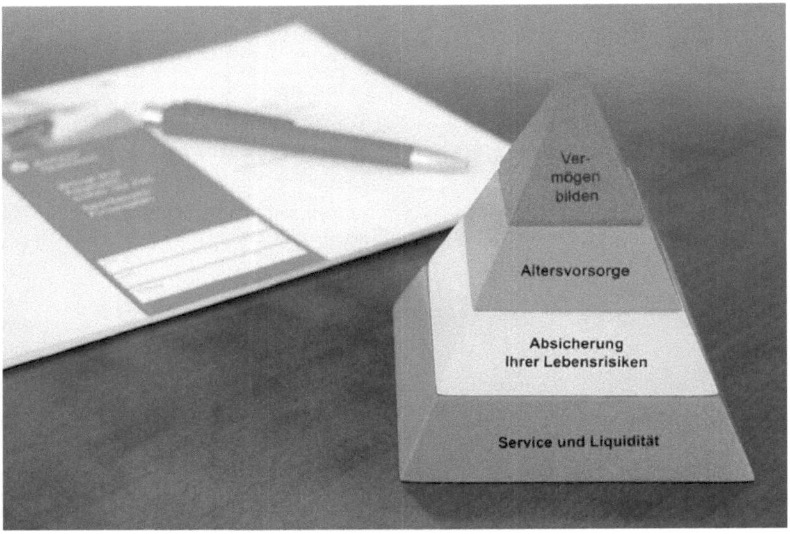

Figure 4: Sparkassen-Finanzkonzept pyramid for private retail banking[98]

The sequence described in the table shows the general consultation approach for the retail banking sector. There are also specialized consultation sequences focusing on

- Savings & asset management
- Retirement provision
- Insurances
- Inheritance

If the customer advisor recognizes a necessity for a specialized consultation, a separate appointment is scheduled and a specialized advisor is most likely consulted.[99]

The official guideline can be considered as the target state of the customer journey[100] or the model of the envisioned state of the journey.[101] In contradiction with the definition provided by the authors quoted, the guideline is not based on an actual customer journey project conducted with empirical research. Consequently,

98 source: Berliner Sparkasse (ed.) (2017), retrieved from http://blog.berliner-sparkasse.de/
99 cf. Sparkassenverlag (ed.) (2013), pp. 58-98
100 cf. Oberholzer / Eichholzer (2017), p. 17 & p. 25
101 cf. Kalbach, J. (2018), p. 213

the research conducted in this paper aims to match the theoretical approach described above with the actual applied and experienced journeys of customers.

4 Empirical Research: Research Methodology

4.1 Gathering Data for CJA

There are several ways financial services providers examine customer satisfaction and process efficiency. Online customer surveys and mystery shoppers are a common way to get an impression on customer satisfaction, while third-party consultant companies provide analysis and reports for the organizational structure and process efficiency to develop improvement proposals.

The data gathering techniques is commonly distinguished in literature in two categories:

- **Quantitative research:** this research method is very common in educational institutions and considers the reality can be representable by utilizing theoretical models. Generally, it is based on objective and reliable data.[102] In other words, quantitative content usually expresses validity through big data volumes.[103] It can be considered representative[104] as it utilizes a large quantity of data to derive general statements.[105]
- **Qualitative research:** this research method aims for exploring reality on the basis of the subjective view of relevant interlocutors. Subsequently, possible causes of their behavior are explored for deeper understanding.[106] Qualitative research does not aim to represent a population or target group with statistical significance, [107] rather it is conducted with limited samples of respondents to get a deeper insight and understanding.[108]

In case of CJA, Kalbach, J. (2018) offers a broad overview of different quantitative and qualitative approaches and sources which are named below. Some examples suitable to the financial industry are added to Kalbach's elaboration.

---

102 cf. Roebken, H. / Weitzel, K. (2016), p. 13 cited from v. Saldern (1992), p. 378

103 cf. Kalbach, J. (2018), p. 145

104 cf. Wolf, S. (2008), p. 9

105 cf. Wolf, S. (2008), pp. 31-32

106 cf. Roebken, H. / Wetzel, K. (2016), p.13 cited from Wolf, B / Priebe, M. (2003)

107 cf. Wolf, S. (2008), p. 9

108 cf. Wolf, S. (2008), pp. 31-32

Quantitative research:[109]

- Usage metrics: transactions of credit cards, how many times a customer logs into their online banking.
- Call center reports: classification of call types, e.g. issues with mobile banking app, payment issues, and reasons for forwarding calls to customer advisors.
- Social media and web monitoring: evaluating the interest of customers topic-related by measuring volume of activities for each topic, also applicable for search engines, e.g. Google.
- Industry benchmarks: relation of checking accounts held and mobile app users.

Qualitative research:[110]

- Direct feedback: obtaining legally obligatory or voluntary consultation protocols.
- Social media and reviews: getting insight from the content of user's posts and reviews.
- Market research and industry reports: third-party surveys administered and field experts' analysis of the industry, e.g. strategic orientation and public relations as well as branch network offering digital channels and its relation to customer satisfaction.
- Internal stake holder interviews: open-question interviews with customer advisors about the amount and purpose of customer queries and complaints.
- Field research: customer interview of customers who open or close a bank account or any other processes customers have experienced. In addition, expert interviews aim to collect knowledge from selected professionals to assist replying to the research question.[111]

A different approach distinguishes analytical (e.g. demographic factors, big data) and anecdotal data (interviews, detail insight).[112] The categorization is similar to

---

109 cf. Kalbach, J. (2018), pp. 128-129 & p. 145

110 cf. Kalbach, J. (2018), pp. 107-123

111 cf. Pfadenhauer, M. (2009), p. 451

112 cf. Salesforce.com incorporated (ed.) (n.d.), retrieved from https://www.salesforce.com/

the quantitative and qualitative categories described, which are more common and are a standard science approach.

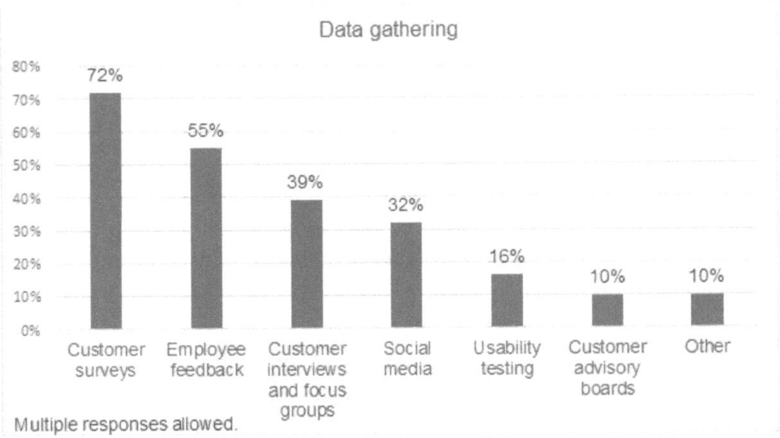

Figure 5: Most common methods of data gathering for CJA[113]

Oberholzer and Eichholzer (2017) recommend qualitative-based customer interviews with a scope of eight customers to attain a valid and reliable customer journey.[114]

Kalbach, J. (2018) sees field research with interviews of participants in the location of their experience as the best technique to investigate hypotheses.[115] Consequently, interviews with customers should be conducted instantly after the actual customer journey to avoid a distortion of the story the customer tells the researcher.

---

113 adapted from Mycustomer / Quadient (eds.) (2018), retrieved from https://www.quadient.com/

114 cf. Oberholzer / Eichholzer (2017), p. 21

115 cf. Kalbach, J. (2018), p. 120

The empirical research in this paper examines actual customer interviews with eight customers for the following reasons:

- CJA are not yet well-established in the financial industry in Germany. Therefore, the potential for helpful outcomes is higher and this paper contributes in developing CJA in the industry.
- CJA have never been conducted at the example institute Sparkasse 1 in its originally defined way.
- Compared to quantitative data, the qualitative approach of customer interviews allows to gain deeper insight into customer experiences as described above.
- An additional expert interview with an executive at the bank analyzed, partially covers employee feedback.
- The customer interview ranks third in the most applied research method of CJM.[116]
- The savings bank already has experience with the two most applied research methods. The following examinations were conducted in the institute previously:
    - Online customer surveys are conducted frequently, mostly every two years.
    - Mystery shoppers are frequently testing the customer experience.
    - Customer advisory boards were implemented temporarily for selected target groups.
- A CJA exclusively based on employee feedback can be misleading and often interpret the assumptions by employees as actual customer experiences.[117] This may result in a distorted picture of the journey, resulting in false inferences and bad recommendations.

116 see figure 5

117 cf. Bodine, K. (2015), retrieved from https://www.qualtrics.com/

4.2 Critical Reflection of Gathering Data through Interviews

Besides the named and described attributes of qualitative research, there are other points of criticism of interview-based research: [118]

- **Lack of background knowledge of researcher:** the interviewer does not usually have the same background knowledge about the topic, which might lead to lack of understanding. However, the researcher of this study can prove to have sufficient background knowledge as he is an expert working in the financial industry.[119]
- **Information flood:** interviews are conducted by means of scheduled appointments, which are limited in time. Information from the interview has the potential to be lost, given the shear amount of information shared by the interviewee which could not be captured completely by the researcher. The post processing is also affected when translating the information from one format to another.
- **Assumptions and biases:** the interviewer can lead the interview in a certain direction which results in a potential conscious or unconscious bias and distortion of the interviewee's actual viewpoint.[120]

It is recommended to validate certain qualitative feedback from the customer journey project by examining the identified issues in a survey or with other quantitative methods. The quantitative validation is statistically necessary to gather reliable data and to gain sight of the big picture.[121]

---

[118] cf. Bimazubute, R. (2005), p. 98

[119] see chapter 1.1

[120] cf. DeFranzo, S.-E. (2014), retrieved from https://www.snapsurveys.com/

[121] cf. Nicastro, D. (2016), retrieved from https://www.cmswire.com/

4.3 Empirical Research: Data Collection

Within this study, empirical research was conducted through qualitative customer and expert interviews.

4.3.1 Expert interviews

Expert: Expert 1, Sparkasse 1

For a deeper understanding of how the comprehensive consultation approach is perceived by sales representatives in the savings banks, a structured expert interview was conducted. The key focus was identifying issues and discrepancies in the application of the approach. The consulted expert is in an executive position and responsible for reaching sales targets in product sales and ensuring that quality standards are met by subordinates.[122] Additionally, the interviewee is also considered as a surrogate for sales representatives.[123] This indirectly covers employee feedback. The savings bank, Sparkasse 1, ensures the application of the approach by implementing it in the sales target map through a quota system for the assigned customer base of each sales representative.[124]

Expert: Expert 2, Sparkasse 2

The Sparkasse 2 is a large savings bank in Germany and currently running a CJA project conducting the bank's consultations of securities and investment products. Expert 2 is a member of the project team. The interview's purpose is to gain insight into the operational application of an actual CJA project in a German savings bank and assist replying to the research questions of this study. The interview examines the concrete application of the CJA. This includes the way it was carried out; the business issues which were addressed; pain and pleasure points; and the results

122 see appendix 7: expert interview Sparkasse 1 for details and full interview (German).

123 cf. Bogner A. / Littig B. / Menz W. (2009), p. 2

124 Background information: the savings bank sets an annual target quota for conducted comprehensive consultations for every sales representative's customer base. For example: 35% of all assigned customers of advisor John Smith had a comprehensive consultation in the last 18 months (situation at December 31 of the previous year). The data is gathered from the CRM system of the bank. The target quota for next year will probably be set to 40%, a 14% increase. The quota captures all customers who experienced a comprehensive consultation during the past 18 months.

and probable consequences for the savings bank running the CJA and their customer journeys in the target vision.[125]

4.3.2 Customer interviews and customer journey maps

To gain insight into actual customer experience, eight in-depth interviews with different customers were led by the author of this paper. The participants were acquired by the author and supported the research voluntarily. They are all customers of a savings bank and experienced at least one comprehensive bank consultation. The interviews were semi-structured with a clear focus on thoughts, perceptions, and positive and negative emotions the customer experienced during comprehensive consultations. The sequence of the interview is illustrated and documented in the appendices.[126] The result: six out of eight interviews provided enough crucial content to create a customer journey map for their respective interviews.

---

125 see appendix 8: expert interview Sparkasse 2 for details and full interview (German).

126 see appendices 1-6: customer interview 1-6

5 Results

This chapter contains the results of the empirical research and verifies the theoretical research of the previous chapters. Consistent and contradictory findings are also examined.

5.1 Expert Interviews

5.1.1 Expert interview Sparkasse 1

The key findings of the expert interview with Expert 1 in regard to the theoretical findings and the research question of this paper are:[127]

Acquisition of appointments:

- The acquisition of an appointment with a customer for any consultation purpose – including comprehensive bank consultations – is most successfully carried out while simultaneously updating customers with existing products in portfolio. Their checking accounts play a key role.
- Frequent product use by customers increases both the opportunities as well as the number of occasions to schedule appointments.
- Simple service requests of customers are exploited and converted to scheduled appointments, e.g. ordering a new debit card, applying for an overdraft facility, customer complaints, etc.

Comprehensive bank consultations:

- Scheduling appointments with the sole focus on providing comprehensive bank consultation is least successful because customers do not see the benefits.
- Despite intensive marketing campaigns, there is almost no active customer demand for comprehensive bank consultations.
- There is no defined process, structure, or guideline applied by sales representatives. The technical process' user-friendliness recently improved, therefore, a guideline is not required. Sales techniques and quality standards are practiced heterogeneously. The expert is not in favor of a homogenous standardization as it inhibits and discourages the advisor in their job.

---

[127] see appendix 7: expert interview Sparkasse 1 for details and full interview (German).

- On the other hand, the expert mentions a homogenous quality in the customer experience – independent from the consulting advisor - as a major advantage of the concept.
- In terms of the advisor's point of view, the concept provides a structure and serves as a reminder for critical points. This is most important for inexperienced advisors.
- There are no significant disadvantages besides the time exposure of documenting and storing the information in the CRM system. The application of the approach by the advisor is not mandatory.

5.1.2 Discussion and evaluation

Matching the findings from the theoretical research with the expert interview, there are three significant points for discussion:

- A standardized application of the comprehensive bank consultation is not consequently enforced. However, according to the expert a consistent quality is even in the customers and bank advisors interest and beneficial.
- The value and helpfulness are neither appreciated by the customer, nor by the advisor in a satisfactory manner. A 'brand awareness' of the Sparkassen-Finanzkonzept does not exist.
- According to chapters 3.1 and 3.2 a frictionless customer experience is demanded by customers and an outcome of recent developments in the industry. In contrast, simple service requests are often exploited to schedule an appointment with an advisor, even though it is not necessary for the specific customer request. A conflict of interests exists. The advisor is caught between scheduling appointments to sell products and ensure customer satisfaction through a frictionless and fast completion of the customer's request.

5.1.3 Expert interview Sparkasse 2

The key findings of the expert interview with Expert 2 in regard to the theoretical findings of this paper are:[128]

[128] see appendix 8: expert interview Sparkasse 2 for details and full interview (German).

Implementation of the CJA project and project goals

- The CJA is part of a major project about customer experience.
- The project was initiated by the managing board of the bank.
- Key project goals for the bank's securities and investment business are: improve customer experience, an increase in the sales of securities and investments for existing and new customers, as well as increasing customer and employee satisfaction.
- The KPIs in their theoretical definition are not considered and measured. The indicators considered are: earnings, customer, and employee satisfaction.
- The actual CJA is run by approximately 11-12 project members.
- The maps of the journeys are illustrated on paper-based walls in the office and additionally in a digital text version.
- The estimated project duration including the final implementation of changes of processes as well as in sales activities is at least eight months.
- A certain business issue to address and solve was not defined.

Data gathering

- The bank conducted semi-structured, in-depth interviews with 30-35 customers and non-customers between 60-90 minutes in length.
- The customers were clustered based on:
    - Branch and online preferences (three categories).
    - Currently holding assets in customer's portfolio as well as securities account hold or previously held by customer (four categories).

Identified pain and pleasure points and main focus

- Pain and pleasure points were mainly identified in regard to the touchpoints of the actual consultation part of the journey.
- Pain points examples: customer felt overwhelmed by duration of appointments and media used. The service for existing customers holding securities in their account was perceived as poor as they felt a lack of care by the bank. Employees plead for frictionless processes and complained about the overwhelming legal requirements.

- Pleasure points examples: customers perceive a recurrent consultation appointment with a qualified customer advisor as beneficial and valuable.

Process of implicating changes as a result of the CJA project

1. A member of the managing board is frequently briefed by the project team about the project results and the resulting improvement proposals. The managing board member approves the initiation of changes before the actual changing process starts.

2. In most cases, the feasibility of the suggested amendments is analyzed before the implementation is presented to the managing board member.

3. Once a suggestion by the project team was approved by the managing board and its feasibility reviewed, the implementations of the amendments are conducted by the responsible primary departments affected. Internal tests are also performed.

4. A pilot phase is conducted with certain sales units and advisors. The insights gained are evaluated and modifications are made.

5. Complete roll-out.

5.1.4 Discussion and evaluation

The CJA project of the Sparkasse 2 matches the theoretical findings of this paper as follows:

- The managing board is directly involved, approves improvement proposals, and ensures that amendments resulting from the project can get implemented successfully as recommended in chapter 3.3.1.
- The number of the interviews matches the recommendations from chapter 2.1.
- The interviews are conducted in the same way and structured the same as evidenced in this study.

The project differs in the following points:

- Neither KPIs, nor a certain business issue were determined; however, general goals were set. According to the success of the project with regard to the results and because the bank has already carried out CJA projects in the past, the precise determination of KPIs and a business issue are not essential. This is particularly not necessary if the project is carried out extensively and in a large-scale regarding scope of research, willingness to change, and deployed resources, e.g. project members. These conditions are met in this case.

- The data gathered was conducted exclusively through qualitative research and not validated by quantitative as stated in chapter 4.2.

Moreover, the interview provides several helpful points from an application-oriented viewpoint which are not contained in the theoretical part of this study. In particular, a detailed process of implicating changes is described. The content-related results of pain and pleasure points as well as the implementations will be considered with the findings of the customer interviews of this study and complemented in the journey map of the target vision below.

5.2 Customer Journey Maps

The empirical research results of this study conducted through in-depth interviews with customers are illustrated in customer journey maps on the following pages. The interview process is described in the interview documentation.[129] The theoretical findings of the previous chapters are applied. The interactions and perceived touchpoints of the customers are chronologically portrayed.[130] Thoughts and feelings to every step are outlined. The customer experience is categorized into pain and pleasure points or classified as neutral on the emotion curve. In addition, exact scrutinized feelings of the customers help to evaluate the perception of the touchpoints. Finally, identified opportunities and problems are derived and illustrated in the lower section of the maps.

5.3 Discussion and Evaluation

The results show that certain experiences and thoughts were mentioned by different customers. The identification of patterns in the behavior, the attitude, and characteristics of interviewed customers can be used to create consolidated customer journey maps with aggregated categories.[131] However, this approach is not applied in this study because a precise classification of the customers in two different categories is not practicable due to the wide variety of customer feedback collected.

---

129 see appendices 1-6: customer interviews 1-6

130 for the derivation of the general elements of the journey maps, see chapter 3.3.2, in particular, p. 19

131 cf. Oberholzer/Eichholzer (2017), pp. 21-22

Additionally, the large scope of the journey examined results in large amounts of data contained in the single journey maps.

The participants are assigned with an NPS and fan attribute as described above. The classifications of the attributes are based on the quantitative count of positive, neutral, and negative emotions expressed during the interview and documented in the maps as well as the subjective evaluation of the researcher.

Name	Initiative	NPS attribute	Fan attribute
Customer 1	Customer	Passive	Sympathizer
Customer 2	Bank	Passive	Sympathizer
Customer 3	Bank	Detractor	Prisoner
Customer 4	Bank	Promoter	Fan
Customer 5	Customer	Detractor	Prisoner
Customer 6	Customer	Passive	Mercenaries

Table 3: Classification of interview participants

The customer journey maps are illustrated on the following pages.[132]

[132] source: own illustration

Customer 1, Age 32, male, logistician, checking account holder, private retail customer for more than 5 years. **Initiative of journey**: customer schedules appointment about contract transfers resulting from an inheritance.

	Pre consultation			Consultation					Follow-up		Long-term	
	Awareness	Schedule	Arrive	Welcome	Contract transfer	Update & Plans	Suggestions	Decision	Online banking	Securities account	Travel insurance	Estate agent
Interactions	Awareness of bank through using checking account, ATM, credit card and mortgage loan.	Schedules appointment at savings bank because of an inheritance and resulting contract transfers. Looks up phone number on Google and calls savings bank branch.	Drives to branch and finds parking spot immediately. Uses parking spots also after business hours.	Approaches service employee and gets welcomed by customer advisor. Consultation is conducted in separate room. Water and coffee are offered.	Customer advisor suggest to to transfer all contracts and products 1:1 to the customer and briefly describes each product.	Customer advisor updates contact details and asks about plans for the future.	Suggestions to improve customer experience are made by advisor: offering online banking and to switch the checking account tariff (cross- and up-selling).	Customer agrees and signs contracts and purchases an access device (TAN) for online banking. He wants to keep product brochure.	Starts using online banking at home.	Tries to check his transferred securities account online, but it is not available in the online banking of the customer. The access requires a separate online account for the provider of the account.	- Customer visits branch to subscribe on a travel health insurance - Known customer advisor speaks to customer, after advisor is called by service employee.	Estate agent got ordered to sell real estate on behalf of customer. Customer sold house before contract with estate agent got established.
Touchpoints	- Branch - ATM	- Call center - Bank's profile on Google.	- Branch - Branch advertisement - ATM	- Service employee - Other customers - Personal advisor - Separate room for consultations - Beverage offer	- Personal advisor - Contracts - Financial portfolio on computer screen.	- Personal advisor	- Personal advisor - Computer - Product brochure paper-based	- Personal advisor - Contract copies - Product brochure paper-based - Access device (TAN)	- Contracts - Welcome letter - Website - Access device (TAN) - Debit card	- Website of partner (Sbroker) - Website - Online banking	- Branch - Branch advertisement - Service employee - Known advisor. - Insurance application (paper-based)	- Estate agent - Phone call
Thoughts and Feelings	*I opened checking account at this bank because I moved. Branch was very close to my place. I am using my checking account frequently. I once took advice from a specialist for mortgage loans. I never got called or contacted by my advisor. I am not in favor of online banks. I am* ***not interested*** *comparing products with other banks.*	*I am glad it is the same bank my relative was customer of. That makes it* ***easier****. The bank does not have a large amount on reviews on Google. I do not really care about that.*	*I appreciate to be a customer of this bank because I can also use their parking spots after business hours. The branch is well designed and I frequently withdraw money at their ATM.*	*I never got so much attention by this bank. They never offered me water or coffee. I feel* ***appreciated and am surprised*** *about the attention.*	*I just transferred the contracts and wanted to decide later what to do with them. I generally* ***trust*** *the bank and the product decisions made previously.*	*I am currently living in a city which does not belong to the business area of the savings bank, but I am frequently visiting the area and want to stay a customer of the bank, because I am* ***too lazy*** *to switch the bank.*	*I* ***appreciate*** *that the advisor asked about my current life situation. Because it enables the opportunity to make suggestions fitting to my situation; e.g. online banking and to switch to a different checking tariff.*	*The advisor used a brochure to explain the product. I want to keep the brochure because I found the advice helpful. I am a little bit* ***concerned*** *how online banking will work for me and if I could do something wrong. I do not care about purchasing the device, because it increases security.*	*At first the handling sounded complicated, but now it works finally and I am* ***happy*** *about the more transparency of my checking account. Checking my account online is* ***more comfortable*** *and gives me a* ***better feeling*** *about my financial status.*	*I do not want to spend time and memorize all the account names and passwords and do not know why there is a separate account name for my securities account.*	*I feel* ***appreciated*** *that the known advisor talks to me and completes the insurance application form with me.*	*Estate agent kept on calling me, but I did not respond. I already told the agent that the job is already finished. The frequent call approaches were really annoying. Agent did not stop call attempts, even when I left them unanswered several times in a row.*

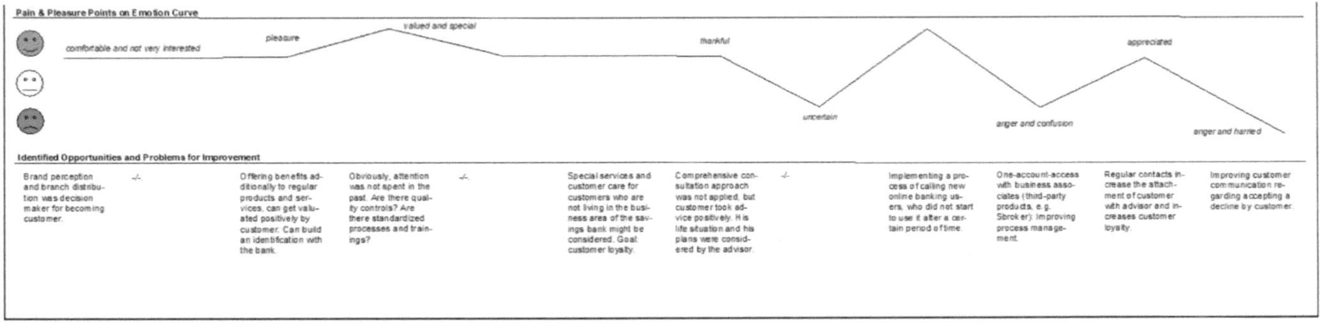

Figure 6: Customer journey map of customer 1

Customer 2, Age 25, male, electronics mechanic, checking account holder, private retail customer for more than 10 years. **Initiative of journey**: customer advisor schedules appointment for comprehensive bank consultation.

	Pre consultation			Consultation					Follow-up		Long-term	
	Awareness	Schedule	Arrive	Welcome & brief chat	Plans & goals	Mapping	Products	Decision	Contracts	Start using	Changes	Frequent use
Interactions	Awareness of bank, advisor and branch by using checking account regularly.	- Ignores an e-mail from customer advisor who suggests a comprehensive bank consultation. - Receives a reminder call and finally schedules an appointment.	- Drives to branch and finding a parking spot instantly. - Tells the employee at the service counter purpose of visit and name of advisor.	- Customer gets immediately welcomed by the advisor at the counter/waiting area and follows advisor to a separate room. - Brief chat - Refusing offer of water or coffee.	- Talks about changes within life: career objectives, future purchase intentions and goals after being asked by advisor.	- A map of all currently hold financial products in the customer's portfolio is created.	- Advisor advices about prepared recommendations.	- Customer selects and agrees on some recommendations and signs contracts: applies for credit card and an investment fund savings plan.	- Receives additional paper-based contracts with mail and stores them in folder. - Receives credit card with mail.	- Purchases items in a retail store with credit card for the first time. - Recognizes debit transactions of investment fund savings plan on account statement online.	- Receives letters about the change of legal requirements or changed terms and conditions.	- Receives monthly or annual statements. - Uses credit card for purchases in retail and online. - Checks account statements online.
Touchpoints	- Branch - ATM - Online-Banking - Website - Befriended with some employees - Service employees	- E-Mail by personal advisor - Phone call by personal advisor	- Parking spots of bank - Branch - Service employee - Service counter - Other customers - Waiting area	- Personal advisor - Separate room for consultations - Beverage offer	- Pyramid of Sparkassen-Finanzkonzept - Personal advisor	- Structure of consultation on computer screen mapping financial portfolio	- Recommendations and contracts (paper-based) - Calculations on computer-screen and paper-based	- Paper-based contracts - Copies are handed out in a folder.	- Paper-based contracts with mail - Credit card with mail	- Credit card in wallet - Online-Banking - Online account statements - Website	- Paper-based mail with terms and conditions	- Paper-based mail - Online-Banking - Website - Online account statements
Thoughts and Feelings	*Using my checking account is* ***comfortable****. I am familiar with the bank and their products. I know and trust my personal advisor.*	*I am* ***not sure if*** *I should schedule an appointment. I think my advisor just wants to sell products. On the other hand, I* ***know and trust the advisor*** *and I have several products of this bank in my portfolio. There might be legal or other changes which* ***can affect*** *the way I am using the products and services.*	*I always find a parking spot and there are never long waiting lines.*	*I always get offered water or coffee.* *It is good to see a familiar person. But I am still* ***uncertain****: I think he mainly cares about the earnings of his bank and less about my personal interests, but* ***I know and trust him,*** *he will probably not endanger his reputation.* *Can I afford more products with a regular payment?*	*The advisor* ***admires*** *that I am holding several financial products in my portfolio and care about my future.*	*It* ***helps*** *me to see all my financial products at a glance, because sometimes I feel lost with all my financial products.*	*I feel* ***uncertain*** *to sign a contract for a long term because I did not compare it with competitors, nor did I some research on the web.* *But spending time on comparing and reading all the terms in detail is* ***disgusting****, as it takes so much time.*	*My former experiences with the bank and the advisor finally* ***encourage*** *me to sign.*	*Why do I get so much paper? I can not spend time on reading all the terms. Does someone actually read that?* *(I am* ***happy*** *finally getting my credit card because I can use it immediately and it looks great in my wallet. Pretty simple and it comes with a simple letter.)*	*I see the debit transactions on my account statements online. Everything seems to be* ***alright.***	*A change of the terms and conditions of my products and services in my portfolio make me feel* ***concerned*** *and let me consider terminating the product.*	*(The credit card gives me more opportunities paying in retail and online.)* *Those annual statements are* ***overwhelming*** *me with all that additional information.* *In addition: I do not follow the social media page of the bank.* ***I am not interested*** *in their sweepstakes.*

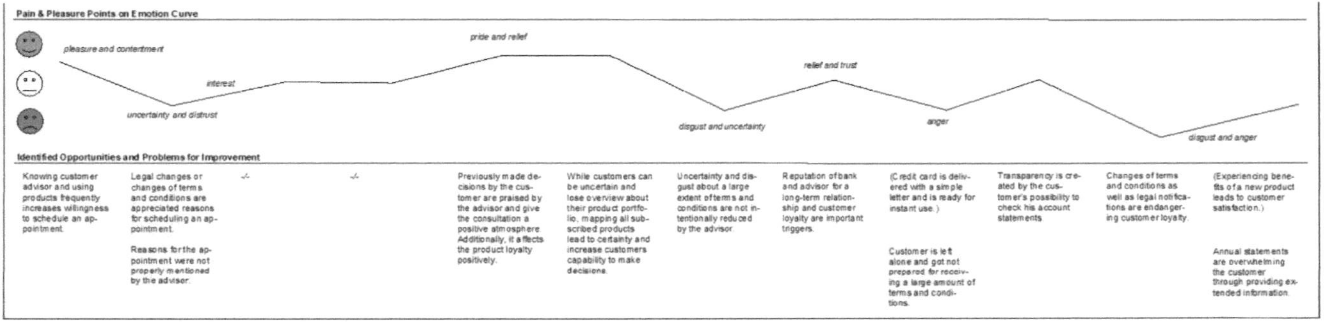

Figure 7: Customer journey map of customer 2

Customer 3. Age 25, female, student, checking account holder, private retail customer for more than 9 years. **Initiative of journey**: customer advisor schedules appointment to update lodged signature sample.

	Pre consultation				Consultation				Long-term			
	Awareness	Schedule	Arrive	Bank employees	Welcome	Consultation	Recommendations	Decision	Online research	Forms	Need	Credit card
Interactions	Awareness of bank, branch and ATM. (No former consultations have been conducted.)	- Customer gets called by a bank employee to schedule an appointment for updating the lodged signature sample. - Customer agrees and schedules appointment.	- Drives to branch and finds parking spot immediately. - Approaches service employee.	- Waits in the waiting area of the service area. - Notices bank employees and recognizes some of them as former schoolmates.	- Advisor approaches customer and introduces himself in the waiting area. - Customer is lead to a separate room for the consultation.	- Customer advisor starts with comprehensive consultation (Sparkassen-Finanzkonzept) - Asks customer about plans in life. - Creates map about financial portfolio	- Customer listens to advisor who is making recommendations, e.g. for a building society contract. - Advisor mentions updating sample signature.	- Finally signs signature card to update lodged signature. - Rejects all recommendations by advisor.	- Friends recommend online banking to customer. - Looks up product information online. - Researches about competitors. - Applies for online banking.	- Gets forms for online banking application with mail. - Signs forms and deposit them in letterbox of branch. - Activates online banking: SMS-authorization.	- Informs herself online whenever she has a need for financial products, e.g. credit card. - Orders credit card online.	- Receives credit card with mail. - Starts to purchase goods in retails with credit card instantly.
Touchpoints	- Branch - ATM	- Phone call - Bank employee.	- Branch - Service employee - Branch advertisement - Waiting area - Other customers	- Waiting area - Employees - Other customers - Branch advertisement	- Personal advisor	- Personal advisor - Computer-based consultation	- Recommendations and offers on the screen and partially paper-based. - Paper-based signature card	- Personal advisor - Offers with e-mail - Offers paper-based. - Paper-based signature card.	- Website - Online banking	- Mail - Online banking form - Website - Online banking - SMS tan authorization	- Website - Online banking - Credit card online application	- Mail - Credit card - Authorization method: „Secure-Code by Mastercard"
Thoughts and Feelings	*I have been customer of this bank since I was a kid. I also joined the Knax-Klub when I was young (kids club by savings bank). My parents were also customers of this bank. That's why I picked the same one. I frequently withdraw cash from the ATM in the branch.*	I think I should agree and schedule an appointment. I do not want to risk any issues which might occur with my checking account in the future. I think it will not take a long time to go there.	*I **do not know** where the customer advisor's office is located, so I decide to talk to a service employee of the bank to seek for assistance.*	*I am **wondering** who got hired by the bank. I recognize some of the employees. They were former schoolmates. That's **interesting** how seriously they are behaving on their job.*	*I am kind of **curious** and **confused** why I get lead to a separate room.*	*I am **concerned** and feel **uncomfortable** because the advisor asks me all these questions, as I was not told the purpose of it. I respond to the questions, because I am polite. I just came here to update my sample signature. The advisor simply asks me one by one about my existing financial products. These are a lot of questions and it is **annoying**.*	*I did not schedule the appointment to expand my financial product portfolio and did not expect the appointment taking such a long time. I politely reject his recommendations. I feel **overwhelmed** and think the advisor is acting rude and intrusive.*	*I am rejecting his offers, did not want to get offers with e-mail and feel **overpowered**.*	*I **prefer** to look up information online instead of consulting an advisor from the bank. I am expecting the advisor trying to give me a hard sell.*	*Friends recommended to get online banking to check my account daily and avoid visiting the branch frequently.*	*I am **glad** that online banking offers the possibility of ordering a credit card directly without the necessity to sign and deposit paper forms. The credit card comes with a low annual fee. Because of the low fee I am not comparing the product offers of the savings bank with competitors.*	*The credit card works **fine**. I am **slightly proud** to have one, as it has a positive image of solvency. But I do not know why I should register for the „SecureCode", and what it means. Seems like it would take some time to register. But what is the purpose of it? It is **confusing** and **not** very **interesting**. I might look it up online later.*

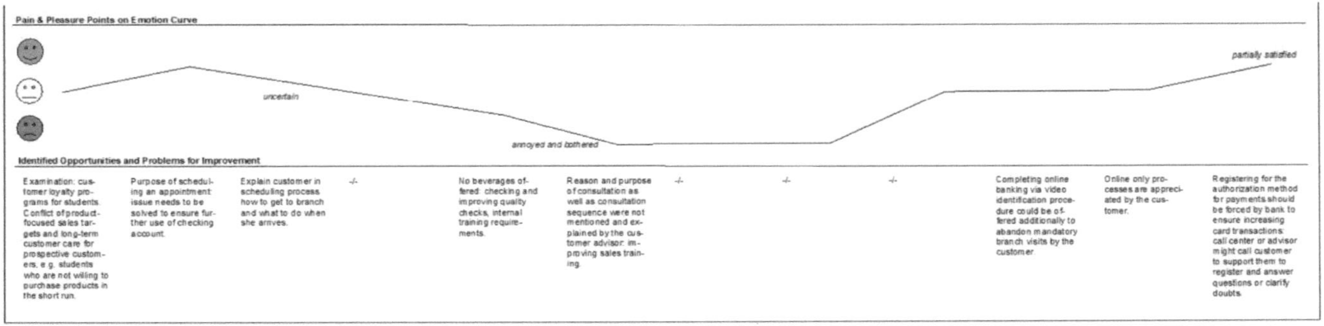

Figure 8: Customer journey map of customer 3

Customer 4, Age 35, male, legal assistant, checking account holder, private retail customer for more than 15 years. **Initiative of journey**: customer advisor schedules appointment because of due date of building society contract in customer's portfolio.

	Pre consultation			Consultation					Follow-up		Long-term	
	Awareness	Schedule	Arrive	Welcome & brief chat	Changes of plans	Customer's topics	Advisor' topics	Decision	Contracts	Debiting account	Changes	Annual check
Interactions	Awareness of bank, advisor and branch by using checking account regularly. Former consultations took place and customer is satisfied. Using online banking and withdraws money frequently from ATM's.	- Receives a call by advisor who suggests an appointment because of the due date of an existing building society contract. - Gets asked to bring contract folder and ring the doorbell.	- Walks to branch: opposite side of employer's building. - Appointment takes place after opening hours, therefore he rings the doorbell. - Advisor introduces him to newly built branch.	- Customer is lead to separate room for consultations. - Brief chat opened by advisor: *"how is life going? Any updates?"* - Accepts offer of coffee.	- Advisor opens by asking about changes within life: plans and goals.	- Customer tells advisor what topics are important to him today. - Customer is prepared and took notes at home. - E.g. interest about a savings plan for new born son.	- Advisor concludes announced matters and issues from customer with prepared topics and offers and makes recommendations.	- Customer selects some recommendations and signs contracts: an investment fund savings plan for son is opened.	- Contract agreement and order confirmation is delivered into mail inbox of customer's online banking. - Customer gets a visible notification in online banking portal.	- Checks transactions overview / account statements online. - Customer notices savings plan debit on his checking account for the first time.	- Does not spend attention to competitor's offers. - Expect the bank to contact him whenever a decision is necessary.	- Uses checking account frequently. - Customer expects to get contacted to schedule a comprehensive bank consultation at least once a year.
Touchpoints	- Branch - ATM - Online-Banking - Website - Personal advisor	- Phone call - Personal advisor - Folder with contracts of financial products.	- Branch - Doorbell - Personal advisor - ATM - Branch advertisement - Newly built branch with modern design.	- Personal advisor - Separate room for consultations with new inventory and IT equipment (PC). - Beverage offers.	- Personal advisor	- Personal advisor - Folder with contracts brought by customer.	- Recommendations and contracts (paper-based).	- Recommendations and contracts (paper-based).	- Website - Online banking - Online banking notification - Mail inbox online banking - Digital contract agreement - Digital order confirmation	- Monthly debit of savings plan on transaction overview / account statement online. - Website - Online banking.	- Customer advisor. - Phone call.	- ATM - Branch - Online banking - Website - Online account statements and transactions overview.
Thoughts and Feelings	*The savings bank has been my* ***principal bank*** *for years. I am a* ***satisfied customer*** *of this bank and own several products and services which I use frequently. I think it makes sense to obtain a consultation annually to check if an action is needed. I have a personal advisor who takes care of me. My previous* ***experiences*** *were* ***very positive.***	I feel **appreciated and valued** that the advisor is calling me. It is a good service and a **pleasure** that the savings bank takes care of my financial products I am holding and contacts me whenever there is an issue or the need to decide on something.	*I found the doorbell instantly, because the advisor described the location of it. I take it* ***granted*** *to get an appointment after opening hours. The advisor presents the re-designed branch and I feel* ***excited*** *to be one of the first customers to visit the branch, as it looks fancy.*	*My personal advisor is well-known by me and* ***likeable***. *We know each other. I am* ***familiar*** *with the advisor. I feel appreciated by the advisor. I think it is important in regard to customer-orientation to get coffee offered but take it for granted. I* ***enjoy*** *coming to a consultation.*	*Neither the sequence of the consultation was explained, nor why the advisor conducts this information. But I respond because I assume the advisor needs to know it for making individual offers.*	*I am very accurate with my financial products and consider having a structure very* ***helpful***. *Whenever I have a matter regarding financial products, I consult the savings bank. Why should I change it? Why should I switch the bank or spend time on comparing? I am* ***happy*** *with this bank. I feel that I get treated* ***fairly***.	*Some of the topics the advisor has mentioned match the issues I had. I* ***enjoy*** *getting different offers to choose from. I think it is* ***good*** *that the advisor prepared some suggestions, as it makes a good impression. I appreciate the time the advisor spent on it.*	*I feel that I am* ***satisfying a need***: *I am taking care for the future of my new born son. It feels like* ***a general good decision.***	*I feel* ***relieved*** *that everything worked out. I am glad that I did not get paper-based contracts. I prefer to get notifications and confirmations online instead. It is* ***easier*** *and more* ***comfortable.***	*I am* ***taking care*** *for the future of my son. I check debits in the transactions overview of the checking account online frequently.*	*It feels* ***comfortable*** *and is a* ***pleasure*** *to know that there is someone taking care of my financial matters.*	*I take my financial issues* ***seriously***. *I think professional advice and advanced services help me to* ***save time***. *As long as I am* ***satisfied*** *with this bank, I will stay a loyal customer.*

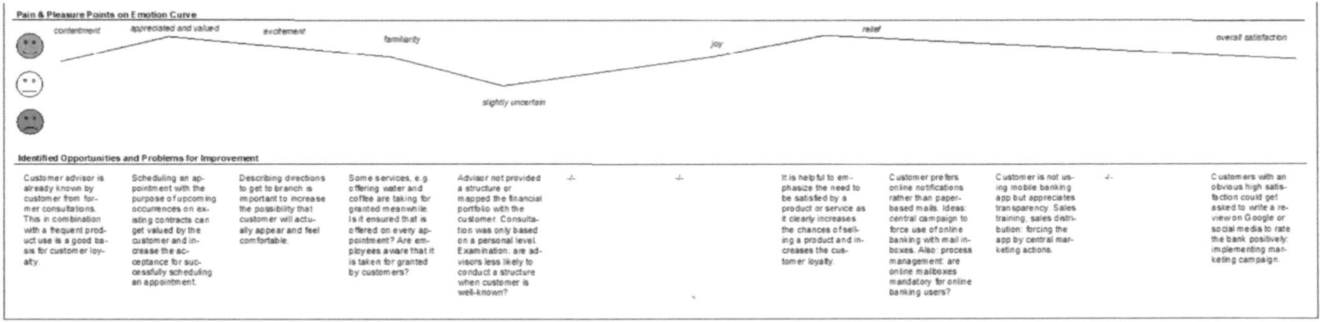

Figure 9: Customer journey map of customer 4

Customer 5. Age 35, male, human resources accountant, checking account holder, private retail customer for more than 15 years. **Initiative of journey**: customer schedules appointment to request a car loan offer.

	Pre consultation			Consultation					Follow-up		Long-term	
	Awareness	Schedule	Arrive	Welcome & brief chat	Changes of plans	Car loan	Recommendations	Decision	Contracts	Debiting account	Increase in price	Online banking limit
Interactions	Awareness of bank, customer advisor and ATM. Customer got a car loan offer from the car dealer previously.	- Customer looks up phone number on business card he got from a previous visit at the branch. - Customer calls bank to schedule appointment and names purpose. - Saves appointment in smartphone cal.	- Branch is close to location of customer and is reached easily. - There are always enough free parking spots available. - Approaches service counter.	- Customer advisor welcomes customer and leads him to separate room. - Accepts offer of coffee. - Brief chat and small talk are started by advisor.	- Advisor starts consultation with asking about changes within life: plans and goals. - *"What has recently changed in your life?"*	- Customer asks for an offer for a car loan. He already got an offer from the car dealer but does not mention it directly. - Customer tells advisor details and receives calculated offer with advice.	- Customer listens to advisor who is making recommendations about insurances. (cross-selling)	- Customer decides on recommendations and signs the contracts.	- Coverage certificate / insurance policy comes 2 weeks after contract was signed with mail.	- Checks transactions overview in mobile banking app routinely. - Recognizes annual fee debit on checking account statement.	- Gets notification from insurance company (business associate of bank) about price rise with annual invoice with mail.	- Calls call center to set a higher limit for online banking transactions. - Asks to speak advisor, but agent responds that advisor is busy and therefore takes care of the issue.
Touchpoints	- Branch - ATM - Online banking - Website - Mobile banking app - Personal advisor	- Phone call - Service employee - Call center	- Branch - Service employee - Branch advertisement - Waiting area - Other customers	- Personal advisor - Separate room for consultations - Coffee	- Personal advisor	- Personal advisor - Paper-based offer	- Recommendations and offers on the computer screen as well as paper-based	- Personal advisor - Offers with e-mail - Offers paper-based - Paper-based contracts	- Coverage certificate / insurance policy - Mail	- Debit on checking account - Mobile banking app - Advertisement on mobile banking app.	- Annual invoice for insurance premium. - Price rise notification	- Call center - Service employee - Mobile banking app
Thoughts and Feelings	*I am **kind of lazy**. That's why I have been customer at this bank for years. It is **just comfortable** for me to stay with this bank. I am **generally satisfied** with this bank. Switching the bank would need effort and time I am not willing to invest.*	I remember that I once got a business card from my personal advisor and stored it at my desk.	*I like to have an appointment at the bank branch. It makes me **feel important** and gives me a good feeling of taking care for my future. I **prefer** to schedule the appointment in the bank branch.*	*The advisor and me already know each other and I feel **respected**. I always look forward to free coffee. I think this is **courteous**.*	*I respond to the questions about my life because I think it is in my interest. It enables the advisor to make individual offers.*	*I do not mention that I already got an offer from the car dealer. I am curious what the bank is going to offer.*	*The customer advisor is really **bothering and annoying** me because the advisor recommends buying a third-liability insurance on every occasion, but I do not want to decide on that. It seems like the advisor does not accept a "no".*	*I finally accept to get coverage how the advisor suggested, because my wife supported the arguments. It covers the whole family. I tell the advisor that I need a day to think about the offer for the loan. Honestly, the interest rates were higher than of the car dealer offer. But I feel **uncomfortable** to mention directly that I already got a better offer.*	*I am **not sure** if I made the right decision to get that insurance coverage. I store the mail and the policy in a drawer of my desk to postpone the decision. I finally forget about it, but still know that I am **not very happy** with that insurance.*	*I pay the annual fee all at once as proposed because there is a concession on annual payment methods. But I still feel **discomfort**.*	*An increase of the annual price comes **totally unexpected**. I think I should **terminate** this contract. But I am just **too lazy** and busy to check a less expensive alternative. I am not in favor of looking up financial topics online, nor I know someone who is an insurance agent.*	*I was expecting that only the customer advisor who knew me, could identify me on the phone and set a new limit. But once the call center agent took care of the issue, I was **happy and positively surprised** that the agent could change it. I got authorized by three security questions about personal details. I feel **relieved**.*

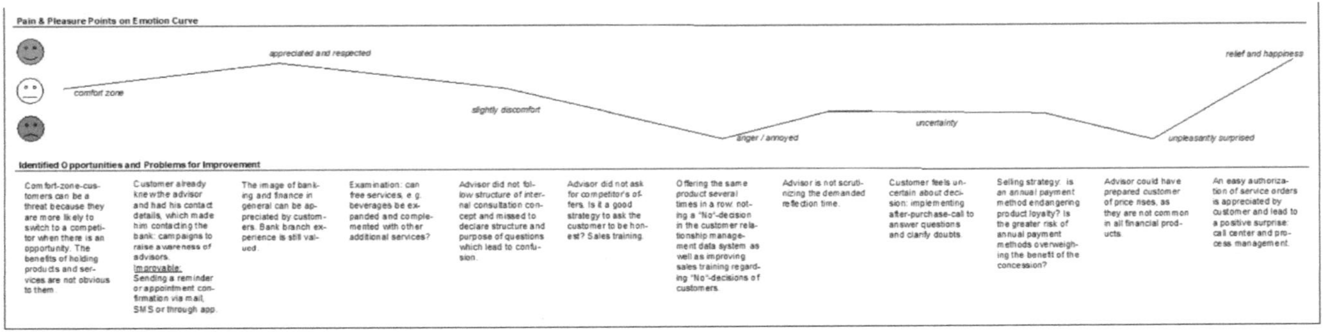

Figure 10: Customer journey map of customer 5

Customer 6, Age 33, male, software engineer, checking account holder, private retail customer for more than 20 years. **Initiative of journey**: customer schedules appointment about contract transfer of mortgage loan from parents.

	Pre consultation			Consultation					Follow-up		Long-term	
	Awareness	Investigate	Schedule	Arrive & Welcome	Offers	Declining	Follow-up appointment	Decision	Calculations	Annual statements	Advisor change	Service request
Interactions	Awareness of bank, advisor and branch by former contact regarding an overdraft facility. Also, customer of an online bank, e.g. using a savings account and credit card.	Comparison portals are conducted to check out competitors and to get prepared for an appointment at the savings bank advisor. Checking website of savings bank as well.	- Customer sends the known advisor an e-mail with offers of dates and reason. - Gets immediate response and finally fixes date.	- 10 Minute drive to Branch. Finding a parking spot immediately. - Approaching service counter. - Gets welcomed by customer advisor and is lead to a separate room.	- Gets offers by customer advisor for transferring mortgage loans from his parents.	- Declines offers of advisor and mentions that he will do the business with an online bank due to the large interest rate difference. - Schedules new appointment on offer of advisor.	- Gets to branch again. - Advisor makes him offers with lower interest rates due to his announcement of switching the bank.	- Customer finally agrees offered contracts and signs. - Customer requests calculations about the loan process to get send with mail afterwards. - Contract copies.	- Receives requested calculations with e-mail	- Receives annual statements with mail. - Filing statements in folder. - Frequently checking counteroffers of competitors and developments.	- Customer receives a paper-based mail stating that he got transferred to an online branch	- Checks his account statement online and notices an unauthorized debit on his checking account. - Checks contact details online & reclaims transact. via WhatsApp.
Touchpoints	- Branch - ATM - Online banking - Website - Mobile app - Bank advisor - Call center	(Savings banks is not available in comparison portals online) - Website	- E-Mail once received by advisor is used to contact the advisor. - Customer advisor replies immediately and schedules a fix appointment date.	- Branch Advertising - Service employee - Other customers - Personal advisor - Separate room for consultations - Coffee/Water offer	- Personal advisor - Contract offers	- Personal advisor	- Branch Advertising - Service employee - Other customers - Personal advisor - Separate room for consultations - Coffee/Water offer	- Personal advisor - Contracts	- E-mail by advisor - Calculations about loan process (credit payments and interest rates)	- Mail - Annual loan account statement - Mobile banking app	- Paper-based mail - Business card with contact details. - Advisors with photo and name in the mail.	- Website mobile - WhatsApp - WhatsApp respond by bank employee
Thoughts and Feelings	*Once I needed a short-term loan and got an overdraft facility. All I had to do was calling the bank advisor. I was* ***positively surprised*** *that a signature was not needed and the limit was available immediately. That experience made me a* ***satisfied*** *customer. But I am aware that savings banks are* ***not low-priced*** *banks.*	*I am pretty sure I will get* ***better offers*** *with better interest rates for mortgage loans online. But I want to give the savings bank a chance to make me an offer as well. The website of the savings bank* ***provides not much information*** *and the savings bank is not available on comparison portals. I precalculate interest rates in total numbers.*	*I remember the advisor from a call some months ago. The advisor sent me an e-mail at that time which is still in my inbox.*	*I already knew the branch and how to get there. But I* ***would have appreciated*** *when the customer advisor would have offered to come to my place instead. I feel* ***comfortable*** *because I remember the advisor who once* ***helped me out*** *on the phone. I take the drink offer and the consultation in a separate room as* ***granted.***	*I was aware that interest rates will be higher compared to the offers from online banks I got, but I am* ***disappointed*** *the difference is higher than expected. I set myself a limit for the difference which is over exceeded by the offers of the savings bank. I have the total numbers I calculated previously in my mind: 200 Euro differences per year is my* ***maximum cap*** *I am ready to accept.*	*I am* ***honest*** *and will mention that I decline the offers. I appreciate to have a personal advisor and advanced services of the savings bank but on the other hand I calculated the actual numbers and that's* ***not worth*** *it. Finally* ***I agree*** *on scheduling a new app. because the advisor once helped me out and I am generally* ***happy*** *with the bank and have been customer for a long time.*	*I feel* ***like I was fooled.*** *The advisor makes better offers because I told the advisor I will switch the bank? That means the first offer was* ***not fair****. I do not want to negotiate about the price, rather I am expecting to get a fair deal offered at the first time.*	*On the other hand, the new offers have lower interest rates, but are still not as low as the counteroffers of the online banks. I finally accept, because my top priority has been to stay customer with this bank. I appreciate the advisor and think it saves time to accept the offer instead of processing it on my own online.*	*I am happy to get the calculations as requested. I am studying the calculations and it matches what the advisor told me.*	*I do not care about the paper-based annual account statements, as I am checking the loan frequently in the mobile app of the bank. The app offers* ***transparent*** *and detailed insight into the loan transactions. I* ***desire to know*** *and check my financial transactions frequently. I also like to be* ***up to date*** *on developments in the market of loans.*	*I* ***wonder*** *why I get transferred to the online branch of the bank and why I get a new advisor. What happened to my former advisor?*	*I already canceled the membership of the club which has debited an amount on my checking account. I am checking the contact details of the bank on my smartphone and am* ***positively surprised*** *that they are on WhatsApp. I finally text them on WhatsApp, get an immediate response and am* ***impressed*** *that they canceled the transaction on behalf of WhatsApp.*

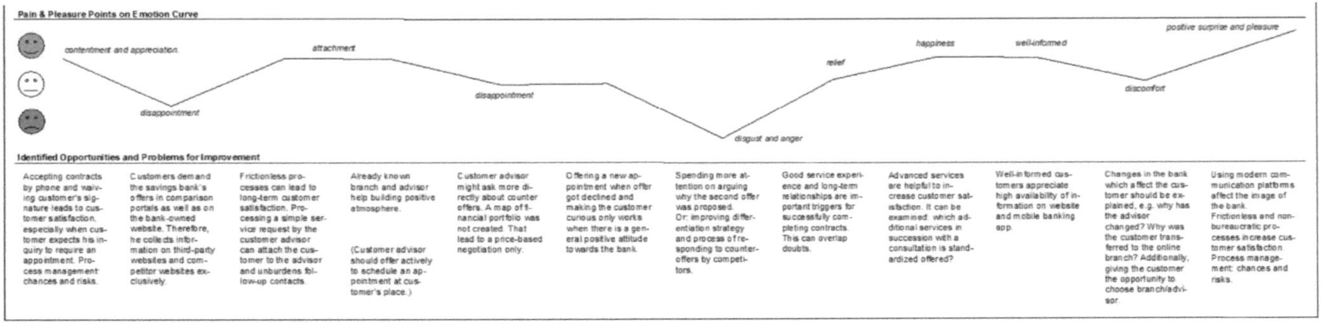

Figure 11: Customer journey map of customer 6

6 Concluding Recommendations

In this chapter, the content-structure and the derivation of the journey map in the target vision (the elements) are described firstly. The map also covers recommendations to implement the adoption to reach the target state. The current state as well as the feasibility of modifications towards the target vision are evaluated. Secondly, the final map is illustrated.

6.1 Mapping the Journey in the Target Vision

- **Sequence and mapping design:** the sequence and different stages of the customer journey[133] as well as the mapping design are derived from the theoretical findings in this paper.[134]
- **Interactions and touchpoints:** the aggregated target vision of interactions and touchpoints are derived and summarized from the findings of empirical research in this study.[135]
- **Managerial Implications and improvement proposals:** this part provides recommendations to reach the target state and improve the KPIs. The current deviation from the target state is evaluated based on conducted customer interviews by determining the count of identified pain and pleasure points or neutral statements by customers for each stage of the journey.[136] This part is supported by the findings from the expert interview with Expert 2, Sparkasse 2.[137]
- **Evaluation of feasibility and effort to adopt proposals:** the required implementation effort and resources to adopt proposals are rated into three categories by the author of this study.
- **Evaluation of central institutions and third-party dependence:** savings banks in Germany are locally managed and, therefore, the percentage of used applications and services of central institutions, business associates and other third-party providers is high. As a result, possible actions to adopt modifications from a CJA project are limited as they often need to be

[133] see chapter 3.4 for the hypothetical customer journey

[134] see chapters 2 and 3.3.2

[135] see appendices 1-6: customer Interviews 1-6 and appendix 8: expert interview Sparkasse 2

[136] see figures 6-11

[137] see appendix 8: expert interview Sparkasse 2

implemented by the central provider or require it take action. For example: the mobile banking app of the savings banks is developed by a third-party company on behalf of the central association of the savings banks. The product management of products from a business associate and the linked communication is within the scope of responsibility of the partner. If improvement proposals are made, they can merely be proposed. A three-step scale is applied and assessed by the author.

- **Research question and KPIs:** the considered journey frames the application of a general comprehensive bank consultation initiated by the bank. In this 'perfect journey', every interaction and touchpoint are pleasure points. To reply to the research question, recommendations based on the conducted CJA are made to improve the perceived value of comprehensive bank consultations as well as improving the customer experience of the journey in general. As a result, the KPIs considered have improved as described in the lower section of the journey map in the target vision. The business issue is solved or minimalized.

6.2 The Customer Journey Map in the Target Vision

The final journey map is illustrated on the next page.[138]

[138] source: own illustration

The journey in the target vision: scheduling and conducting comprehensive bank consultations with a follow-up and long-term part.

	Pre consultation			Consultation					Follow-up		Long-term	
	Awareness	Schedule	Arrive	Welcome & brief chat	Plans & goals	Mapping	Recommendations	Decision	Contracts	Start product use	Changes	Annual check
Interactions	Awareness of bank, advisor and branch by former consultations and frequent product use. The perceived value of bank consultations is based on positive experiences.	- Preannouncement of call is made. - Receives a call and is invited to schedule an appointment. Proper reasons are named. - Customer receives an appointment confirmation via mobile app.	- Gets to known branch and finds parking spot immediately. - Approaches service employee, waits shortly and gets welcomed by known personal advisor who leads to separate room.	- Beverages are offered. - Brief chat opened by advisor: *"how is life going? Any updates?"* - Sequence and goal of today's consultation is explained and illustrated through SFK media.	- Advisor asks about changes within life: career objectives, future purchase intentions and goals. Notes are made. - Customer tells advisor which matters are important. Topics are noted by advisor.	- Benefits and value of creating a map of all currently hold financial products in the customer's portfolio are explained. - Map is created and includes also products hold at competitors.	- Advisor matches prepared recommendations with findings of today and recommends products or modifications. - Benefits for customer based on life goals are explained.	- Advisor uses only legally required terms and conditions, contracts & product sheets. - Advisor mentions possible price adjustments and changes in future. - Is asked to write Google review.	- Contract agreement / order confirmation is delivered into inbox of customer's online banking. - If necessary: Receives short paper-based mail, e.g. delivering credit card.	- Recognizes new product and transactions online. - Receives call or e-mail with offer to assist in starting to use the product & clear questions. - Recommends bank to friends / Writes review on Google.	- Amendments of terms, conditions and legal requirements are digitally delivered in online banking inbox. - Assistance is offered through call or mail. - Appointment might be scheduled.	- Uses payment products frequently. - Customer is contacted by bank to schedule a comprehensive bank consultation at least once a year. - Spends less attention to competitors offers.
Touchpoints	- Branch, ATM, credit card, etc. - Online-Banking - Mobile App - Website - Personal advisor - Annual comprehensive bank consultations	- Pre-notification about call with mail, e-mail or via mobile app. - Phone call made by personal advisor or another bank employee via phone. - Mobile app	- Branch - Branch advertisement - Service employee - Other customers - Personal advisor - Separate room for consultations.	- Personal advisor - Separate room for consultations with IT equipment (PC, TV, tablet, etc.). - Beverage offer - Use of media to illustrate consultation sequence.	- Personal advisor - Paper-based or computer-based documentation.	- Personal advisor - Computer-based mapping	- Product offers: - Recommendations and calculations (digital) on computer screen, sent with e-mail or delivered into online banking inbox of customer for later retrieval.	- Contracts are signed on digital advice. No paper-based copies are handed out.	- Website - Mobile app - Online banking inbox - Digital contract - If necessary: short paper-based mail	- Product appears in online banking. - Transaction/Debit - E-mail - Phone call by personal advisor (recommended) or employee of central outbound call center. - Friends / Google.	- Customer advisor (recommended) or employee of central outbound call center. - Online banking inbox - Mobile app	- ATM, branch and advertisement - Credit card - Online banking - Mobile app - Website - Comprehensive bank consultation with media. - Facebook posts
Managerial implications and improvement proposals to reach target state (High deviation from target state. Medium deviation from target state. Low deviation from target state.)	Ensuring a personal introduction and reach awareness of customer advisor. Alternatively, sending an introduction letter with picture and contact details of advisor. A simple service processed or a call made with exclusive information are good investments to establish a connection between customer and advisor. This can be reached by central campaigns or advisor-based contact goals (CRM).	**1.** Implementing a pre-notification of the upcoming call attempt to schedule an appointment. To avoid customers feeling negatively surprised. **2.** Customers acknowledge the value of a qualified consultation (pleasure point). But the benefits of comprehensive consultations are not appropriately emphasized by advisors in this stage. Improving the sales training as well as introducing a guideline to reach standardized quality are recommended.	**1.** Introducing a digital appointment confirmation via mail / mobile app with directions and required documents to provide by customer on appointment. **2.** Special services for customers who moved and currently not live in the business area of the bank can be considered to improve customer loyalty, e.g. transferring customer to online branch with possibility of video consultation and other digital channels.	It is recommended to improve the sales training and introduce a guideline to ensure advisors follow the defined consultation sequence and use the related media. The goals of the appointment and the reasons for the structure should be clearly named. The duration of the appointment should be named as well.	Link between conducting information about personal life and consultation should be explained and implemented into guideline.	The focus on the comprehensive mapping of all products in customer's portfolio should be enforced through speaking more honestly about products hold at competitors and possible counteroffers.	Customers feel overwhelmed when confronted with a large amount of additional information and media. This can be reduced by limiting the media used to the legally necessary documents. In addition, the forcing of delivering offers, contracts as well as terms and conditions to the inbox of the customer's online banking will transform a pain to a pleasure point.	**1.** To increase product loyalty and customer satisfaction: advisor mentions possible price rises and changes in the future. Implementation in sales training and guideline. **2.** Sales training improvement with regard to declined offers by customer. **3.** Actively addressing "Fan"-customers to write review by implementing a stage in guideline. **4.** Generally: the use of digital solutions is appreciated.	**1.** Paper-based copies should be abandoned to release the customer from document storage at home. Instead, any documents should be delivered into the customer's online banking inbox. **2.** Whenever a paper-based letter is necessary nevertheless, it should be kept as short as possible. A registration for online banking and technical process improvements help to create pleasure points. **3.** Additionally, online banking should be promoted further.	Implementing a process to contact customers in the after-sales stage to increase customer satisfaction and ensure an active product usage. This can be implemented by setting an automatic reminder for the customer advisor (recommended) or alternatively been processed by a central call center. Examples: receiving credit card, first log-in online banking or introducing new authorization methods affecting the customer's currently hold products.	**1.** The design of sales goals can get modified to consider the cancellation of products. This adjustment aims for increasing the customer advisor's effort to improve product loyalty. Possible conflicts of interest or silo mentalities need to be addressed. **2.** Central campaigns to contact customers who are affected by price rises or other changes can get carried out with the same goal (both to be initiated by the sales distribution unit).	**1.** The active use of payment products can be reached through central campaigns based on data analytics, e.g. promotions with regard to transactions. **2.** Communication and particularly advertisement is reduced to certain topics to avoid the customer feeling overwhelmed. **3.** Customer is contacted – even if unfavorable developments of the products in customers' portfolio occurred.

Evaluation of feasibility			**+++ High feasibility rating ++ Medium feasibility rating + Low feasibility rating**								
+++	++	++	+++	+++	++	++	1-3: +++; 4: +	++	++	+	++
Evaluation of effort to adopt proposals			**+++ Low effort rating ++ Medium effort rating + High effort rating**								
++	++	++	+++	+++	+++	++	1-3: ++; 4: +	1-2: +; 3: ++	++	1: ++; 2: +	1: +; 2: ++; 3: ++
Evaluation of central institutions and third-party dependence			**+++ Low dependence ++ Medium dependence + High dependence**								
+++	1: ++; 2: +++	++	+++	+++	++	+	1-3: +++; 4: +	1: +; 2: ++; 3; +++	+++	+	1: ++; 2: +; 3: +
Impact on key performance indicators (KPI)											
Raising awareness of personal advisor and establishing a positive customer relationship increase the **RR**. If the quality of service surpasses customer's expectations, the **NPS** is improved.	The professional initiation of appointments forms the basis for the opportunity to sell products successfully in the actual consultation. That requires a positive attitude by the customer. **CR** is improved.	**1.** improves **CR**. **2.** Frictionless channel use and process implementation improve the **CES**.	A professional introduction to a consultation frames and provides information what to expect. The atmosphere is positive and the chances of completing a product sale increase. The **CR** is improved.	Whenever information is obtained from customers, arguments have to be named beforehand. The **CR** is improved.	The comprehensive mapping of all financial products hold in customer's portfolio makes individual recommendations possible and enables to target competitor's products in customer portfolio. The **CR** is improved.	Improving the customer experience by abandoning paint points impacts the **UX** and **CES** when customer's effort in the pre-consultation and follow-up stages are minimized.	**1.** Increasing the product loyalty enables to sell additional products: **RR, CLV.** **2.** Positive long-term relationships improve **RR** and **CLV**. **3. NPS** is considered. **4.** Process management affects **CES**.	Frictionless processes improve the **CES**.	Ensuring that customers actually use their products to respond to their actual needs and wants improve the **UX** and **RR**. Surprisingly positive service experiences, improve the **NPS**.	A long-term product use increases the **CLV** by reducing the churn rate.	1. Active product usage provides opportunities to schedule appointments: **RR.** 2. Strategic media use increases **CR**. 3. Addressing issues proactively reduces churn rate and increases **CLV**.

Figure 12: The journey map in the target vision

7 Conclusion and Critical Reflection

The theoretical findings and the empirical research answered the research question and helped to solve the defined business issue. Firstly, the outcomes are summarized and evaluated in this chapter. Secondly, the research design is reflected critically.

To summarize the **content-based key outcomes**, customer's perception of the comprehensive bank consultation approach is low due to a lack of practical application of the theoretical concept by sales representatives.[139] In particular, the actual concept and associated media is not emphasized properly by sales representatives to create a satisfactory brand awareness of the Sparkassen-Finanzkonzept. Generally spoken, the design of sales goals, the pursuing by supervisors and the prioritization in sales trainings are points of intersection to improve the perceived value. However, customers clearly recognize and appreciate the value and the benefits of qualified bank consultations. But the perceived value is mainly triggered by the awareness of the brand Sparkasse itself and in particular the relationship with the personal advisor. Managerial implications provided in this study aim for improving the customer experience with regard to the considered KPIs, mainly focusing on the churn and retention rate as they are strategic key targets of the Sparkassen-Finanzkonzept. Key focus points at a glance are:

- Design of sales goals to reach coherent touchpoint perception.
- Sales training to improve customer communication and reach brand awareness.
- After sales stage regarding communication management to reach customer loyalty.

A critical review of the **research design**, and conducted customer interviews in particular, implicates, that a greater scope of customers distinguished in different target groups and demographic factors, would improve the reliability and significance of the gathered data to address an identified business issue more precisely.

The empirical research indicates that a very accurate and limited focus in the research part of a CJA project is less practicable due to the wide variety and

139 In addition, the study shows that the approach lacks an integration of digital solutions, e.g. integrating the mobile banking app in the scheduling process or providing information about former and upcoming consultations in the customer's online banking application. However, the examination of the approach's current status of digitization was not subject of this study.

uncertainty of experiences the customers presumably report in the interviews. Insights into the customer experience through interviews will possibly uncover business issues which the bank was not aware of when implementing the project. Spending more effort on selecting and acquiring interviewees and conducting a brief pre-interview ahead to determine past experiences of the customer, can improve the capability of targeting the business issue more accurately.

Additionally, the background knowledge of CJA project members can distort the research through assumptions and unconscious biases, especially when they are employees of the examined bank. On the other hand, industry-relevant background knowledge is pivotal to carry out an analysis, especially in regard to the characteristics of certain complex customer journeys of the financial industry. A neutral and professional analysis can be reached by a collaboration with a third-party organization in the issue discovery and data gathering stage. If carrying out the CJA project exclusively with own employees, the objectivity can be enhanced by ensuring that participating employees are not involved in the operational application of the examined journeys.

With regard to **further research**, certain expressed perceptions of customers in this study should be validated through quantitative data. In addition, scope and research design of a CJA project should be determined on behalf of the managing board to match their expectations on data quality and enable managerial decisions derived from the project later on. Furthermore, an analysis of the experiences and perceptions of sales representatives can assist replying to the research question further.

Reference List

Alawad, N. / Ragheb, M. / Tantawi, P. (2018): Improving customer experience through customer journey analysis (CJA) of mobile and fixed broadband services in Egypt, in: The Business and Management Review, vol. 9, no. 3, pp. 22-34, 7th International Conference on Business and Economic Development (ICBED); 9-10 April 2018, NY, USA

Becker, R. / Neitzke, G. (2016): Das Fan-Prinzip, in: Diebank, No. 5, vol. 2016. Retrieved December 1, 2018 from https://forum-mainz.de/wp-content/uploads/2016/07/20160501_die-bank_Das-Fan-Prinzip.pdf

Berliner Sparkasse (editor) (2017): Fuer alle Lebenslagen: Was es mit der Pyramide auf sich hat. Retrieved November 17, 2018 from http://blog.berliner-sparkasse.de/fuer-alle-lebenslagen-was-es-mit-der-pyramide-auf-sich-hat/

Bimazubute, R. (2005): Die Nachbereitung von Experteninterviews im expertenzentrierten Wissensmanagement. Doctoral dissertation. Technische Fakultaet der Universitaet Erlangen-Nuernberg, Erlangen

Bodine, K. (2015): Journey Mapping Q&A: How to Research for Customer Journey Maps. Retrieved November 26, 2018 from https://www.qualtrics.com/blog/journey-mapping-qa-how-to-research-for-customer-journey-maps/

Bodine, K. (2018): The customer journey does not equal the customer lifecycle. Retrieved December 6, 2018 from https://kerrybodine.com/the-customer-journey-does-not-equal-the-customer-lifecycle/

Bogner A. / Littig B. / Menz W. (2009) Introduction: Expert Interviews — An Introduction to a New Methodological Debate, in: Bogner A. / Littig B. /Menz W. (editors) Interviewing Experts. Research Methods Series. Palgrave Macmillan, London

Catlin, T. / Duncan, E. / Fanderl, H. / Lorenz, J.-T. (2017): The growth engine: Superior customer experience in insurance, in: McKinsey&Company (editor) (2017): Customer experience: New capabilities, new audiences, new opportunities, pp. 26-35. Retrieved November 20, 2018 from https://www.mckinsey.com/featured-insights/customer-experience

Cavallone, M. (2017): Marketing and Customer Loyalty. The Extra Step Approach, Springer, Cham

Cermak, C. (2018): How Germany's three-tiered banking system works. Retrieved November 13, 2018 from https://global.handelsblatt.com/finance/how-germanys-three-tiered-banking-system-works-779275

Cluster, L (2018): Mapping the way: improve the customer experience with customer journey maps. Retrieved September 26, 2018 from http://asq.org/quality-progress/2018/05/customer-experience-management/mapping-the-way.html

Court, D. / Elzinga, D. / Mulder, S. / Vetvik, O. (2009): The consumer decision journey. Retrieved October 6, 2018 from https://www.mckinsey.com/business-functions/marketing-and-sales/our-insights/the-consumer-decision-journey

DeFranzo, S.-E. (2014): Advantages and Disadvantages of Face-to-Face Data Collection. Retrieved November 27, 2018 from https://www.snapsurveys.com/blog/advantages-disadvantages-facetoface-data-collection/

Deloitte Development LLC (editor) (2017): 2018 Banking Outlook. Accelerating the transformation. Retrieved October 17, 2018 from https://www2.deloitte.com/content/dam/Deloitte/global/Documents/Financial-Services/gx-fsi-dcfs-2018-banking-outlook.pdf

Deutsche Bundesbank (editor) (2017): Payment behavior in Germany in 2017. Fourth study of the utilization of cash and cashless payment instruments, Frankfurt am Main

Deutscher Sparkassenverlag GmbH (editor) (2013): Beraterhandbuch zur Sparkassen-Finanzplanung privat. DSV 293 084 004 / 01.2013, Stuttgart

Deutscher Sparkassen- und Giroverband (editor) (2018): Fokuspapier: Kundenbeduerfnisse aendern sich – Sparkassen entwickeln Filialnetz weiter. Retrieved November 17, 2018 from https://www.dsgv.de/bin/servlets/sparkasse/download?path=%2Fcontent%2Fdam%2Fdsgv-de%2Fpositionen%2Fdownloads%2F180516-DSGV-FP-Entwickl.-SPK-Filialnetze.pdf&name=Sparkassen%20entwickeln%20Filialnetz%20weiter.pdf

Dorfleitner, G. / Hornuf, L. (2016): The FinTech Market in Germany. Final Report October 17, 2016. Retrieved November 13, 2018 from http://www.bundesfinanzministerium.de/Content/EN/Standardartikel/Topics/International_affairs/Articles/2016-12-13-study-fintech-market-in-germany.pdf?__blob=publicationFile&v=2.

The Economist (editor) (2017): ING, a Dutch bank, finds a winning digital strategy. Retrieved November 13, 2018 from https://www.economist.com/finance-and-economics/2017/11/09/ing-a-dutch-bank-finds-a-winning-digital-strategy

Ernst & Young (editor) (2016): EY Global Consumer Banking Survey 2016. Retrieved November 13, 2018 from https://www.ey.com/Publication/vwLUAssets/ey-global-consumer-banking-survey-2016-pressegespraech/$FILE/ey-global-consumer-banking-survey-2016-pressegespraech.pdf

Ernst & Young (editor) (2016b): Winning the battle for relevance. 2016 Global Consumer Banking Survey 2016. US Executive Summary. Retrieved November 13, 2018 from https://www.ey.com/Publication/vwLUAssets/EY-global-consumer-banking-survey-us-executive-summary/$FILE/EY-global-consumer-banking-survey-us-executive-summary.pdf

Ernst & Young (editor) (2017): Germany Fintech Landscape. Retrieved November 12, 2018 from http://www.ey.com/Publication/vwLUAssets/ey-germany-fin-tech-landscape- 2017/$FILE/ey-germany-fin-tech-landscape.pdf

Forum Marketing- und Kommunikationsberatung GmbH (Edtior) (n.d.): Was ist das Fan-Prinzip?. Retrieved December 1, 2018 from https://forum-mainz.de/fan-prinzip/

GFT Technologies (editor) (2017): Banking Expert Survey 2017, London

GfK Crossmedia Link (editor) (2017): Customer Journey Banking. ROPO-Studie fuer Bankprodukte in Deutschland. Management Summary. Retrieved November 20, 2018 from https://www.thinkwithgoogle.com/intl/de-de/insights/markteinblicke/neue-studie-uber-banking-im-digitalen-zeitalter-radikaler-wandel-im-konsumentenverhalten/

Gingiss, D. (2018): How company silos can destroy the customer experience. Retrieved December 13, 2018 from https://www.forbes.com/sites/dangingiss/2018/08/15/how-company-silos-can-destroy-the-customer-experience/#40791de46968

Gleeson, B. (2017): Why silos kill the ability to communicate a unified vision, and 5 ways to eliminate them. Retrieved December 13, 2018 from https://www.forbes.com/sites/brentgleeson/2017/06/20/why-silos-kill-the-ability-to-communicate-a-unified-vision-and-5-ways-to-eliminate-them/#2c11e44929a4

Glenn, R. (n.d.): Digital Marketing Strategy. 6 KPIs of Customer Experience in Financial Services. Retrieved November 28, 2018 from https://www.digitalagent.com/6-kpis-of-customer-experience/

Groenroos, C. (2012): Conceptualising value co-creation: A journey to the 1970s and back to the future, in: Journal of Marketing Management, 28:13-14, pp. 1520-1534, DOI: 10.1080/0267257X.2012.737357

Henk, A / Holthaus, J.-U. (2015): Herausforderungen – Zukunftsorientierte Neuausrichtung des Vertriebs von Banken und Sparkassen, in: Brock, H / Bieberstein, I. (editors) (2015): Multi- und Omnichannel-Management in Banken und Sparkassen. Wege in eine erfolgreiche Zukunft. Springer, Wiesbaden, pp. 61-73

Holmlid, S. / Evenson, S. (2008): Bringing service design to service sciences, management and engineering: in Hefley, B. / Murphy, W. (editors), Service Science, Management and Engineering Education for the 21st Century, vol. 3, Springer Science & Business Media, New York, NY, pp. 341-345.

Horváth & Partners Management Consultants (editor) (2015): Studienbericht. Multikanalvertrieb in Zeiten der Digitalisierung. Online, offline und Hybrid. 2015. Sales Performance Excellence in Financial Industries. Retrieved November 17, 2018 from https://www.horvath-partners.com/fileadmin/user_upload/Multikanalvertrieb_2015_Studienbericht_web-g.pdf

International Business Machines Corporation (editor) (n.d.): Omnichannel banking. From transaction processing to optimized customer experience. Retrieved November 21, 2018 from https://www.ibm.com/industries/banking-financial-markets/resources/omnichannel-banking-paper/

Investopedia (editor) (n.d.): Silo Mentality. Retrieved November 21, 2018 from https://www.investopedia.com/terms/s/silo-mentality.asp

Investors Marketing Management Consultants (editor) (2016): Wachstum der Direktbanken haelt an. Retrieved November 13, 2018 from http://www.investors-marketing.de/data/immc/media/doc/20170710_PM_Direktbanken.pdf

Kalbach, J. (2018): Mapping Experiences: A complete guide to creating value through journeys, blueprints & diagrams. Seventh edition. O`Reilly Media, Inc., Sebastopol, CA.

Kaplan, K. (2016): When and how to create customer journey maps. Retrieved September 29, 2018 from https://www.nngroup.com/articles/customer-journey-mapping/

Kazmierczak, F. / Jelinski, J. (n.d.): 15 KPIs to track for E-Banking and Mobile Banking. Retrieved December 1, 2018 from https://campaign.piwik.pro/15-kpis-track-e-banking-wp/?pk_vid=96d3b9e7d72af53d1543676483bc059c

Kazmierczak, F. / Jelinski, J. (n.d.) (b): 6 Steps to Start Capturing Customer Journey in e-Banking an m-Banking. Retrieved December 1, 2018 from https://campaign.piwik.pro/6-steps-start-mapping-customer-journey-e-banking-wp/

Koch, P. / Floetotto, M. / Weigl, U. / Schroeck, G. (2016): The road ahead. Perspectives on German banking. German Banking Practice March 2016. Retrieved November 14, 2018 from https://www.mckinsey.com/~/media/McKinsey/Industries/Financial%20Services/Our%20Insights/The%20road%20ahead%20Perspectives%20on%20German%20banking/The-road-ahead-Perspectives-on-German-banking.ashx

Levey, Y. (2014): A Multi-Channel Strategy for Banks. Retrieved November 22, 2018 from https://www.slideshare.net/yaellevey/multichannel-strategy-v01

Maechler, N. / Naeher, K. / Park, R. (2016): From touchpoints to journeys: seeing the world as customers do. Retrieved September 25, 2018 from https://www.mckinsey.com/business-functions/marketing-and-sales/our-insights/from-touchpoints-to-journeys-seeing-the-world-as-customers-do

McKinsey & Company (editor) (2017): Retail Banking Insights: The Winning Formula for Omnichannel Banking in North America. Retrieved November 22, 2018 from https://www.mckinsey.com/industries/financial-services/our-insights/the-winning-formula-for-omnichannel-banking-in-north-america

Meroni, A. / Sangiorgi, D. (2011): Design for Services. Gower.

Mycustomer / Quadient (editors) (2018): Customer journey mapping research report 2018. A global study examining maturity and best practices. Retrieved November 21, 2018 from https://www.quadient.com/resources/mycustomers-2018-customer-journey-mapping-research-report

Nguyen, P. / Pupillo, N. (2012): Branded Moments - Vom zufaelligen Kundenerlebnis zur aktiven Gestaltung von Wow- Momenten in der Kundenintegration bei Vodafone Deutschland: in: Manfred Bruhn / Karsten Hadwich (editors): Customer Experience. Forum Dienstleistungsmanagement. Wiesbaden, pp. 317-330.

Nicastro, D. (2016): 7 steps to customer journey mapping. Retrieved December 6, 2018 from https://www.cmswire.com/customer-experience/7-steps-to-customer-journey-mapping/

Oberholzer, G. / Eichholzer, A. (2017): Customer journeys: Kunden verstehen und mit phaenomenalen customer journeys uebersaettigte Maerkte erobern. Fifth edition. Epubli Gmbh, Berlin.

Ollmann, M. / Pramann, J.-A. (2016b): Fintech in Deutschland - Eine Bestandsauf- nahme: Die Marktdurchdringung von deutschen Fintech-Unternehmen, in: Corporate Finance, vol. 7, pp. 95-98, CF1195684

Pfadenhauer, M. (2009): Das Experteninterview: Ein Gespraech auf gleicher Augenhöhe, in: Buber, R. / Holzmueller, H.-H. (editor): Qualitative Marktforschung. Konzepte - Methoden - Analysen. Second Edition, Wiesbaden, pp. 449-462.

Plettenberg, P. / Kaucic, A. (2016): Cultivating the Customer Relationship in Banking. Retrieved December 14, 2018 from https://www.at-kearney.it/documents/10192/8569835/Cultivating+the+Customer+Relationship+in+Banking.pdf/93efddd4-3eae-44ca-a7f6-cbf1b9f18edd

Röbken, H. / Wetzel, K. (2016): Qualitative und quantitative Forschungsmethoden. 2nd edition. Carl von Ossietzky Universitaet, Oldenburg

SAS Institute Inc. (editor): Customer Experience Management: What it is and why it matters (n.d.). Retrieved September 28, 2018 from https://www.sas.com/en_us/insights/marketing/customer-experience-management.html

Salesforce.com incorporated (editor) (n.d.): Customer Journey Maps: How to Guide Your Leads to Customers. Retrieved December 6, 2018 from https://www.salesforce.com/products/marketing-cloud/best-practices/customer-journey-maps/

Sauro, J. (2015): Customer analytics for dummies. John Wiley & Sons, Inc. Hoboken, New Jersey

Schwarz, M. / Dapp T.F / Beck, G.W. / Khussainova, A. (2017): Branch closures: German banks are shifting up a gear amid Herculean challenge of digitisation. Retrieved November 13, 2018 from https://www.kfw.de/PDF/Download-Center/Konzernthemen/Research/PDF-Dokumente-Fokus-Volkswirtschaft/Fokus-englische-Dateien/Fokus-2017-EN/Fokus-No.-181-October-2017-Branch-of-banks.pdf

Segelstroem, F. (2013): Stakeholder engagement for service design: How service designers identify and communicate insights. PhD thesis. Linkoeping, Sweden: Linkoeping University Electronic Press.

Soldwedel, A. / Inhoffen, L. (2018): Internetriesen draengen in den Bankenmarkt. Google, Amazon, Facebook und Apple veraendern den Finanzsektor. Retrieved November 20, 2018 from https://yougov.de/news/2018/06/12/gut-jeder-funfte-kann-sich-vorstellen-finanzproduk/

Sparkassen- und Giroverband Hessen-Thueringen (editor) (2018): Sparkassen-Finanzkonzept Private Kunden. Fachseminar Vertriebssteuerung Eppstein. 19. Februar 2018. Documents for participants and presentation slides.

Reference removed due to policy on data protection.

Strudley, C. (2015): KPI's for Banking & Finance – Is Customer Effort Score the best measure for predicting loyalty? Retrieved December 1, 2018 from https://futurethinking.com/blog/news/kpis-for-banking-finance-is-customer-effort-score-the-best-measure-for-predicting-loyalty/

The interaction design foundation (editor) (2018): The principles of service design thinking – building better services. Retrieved September 29, 2018 from https://www.interaction-design.org/literature/article/the-principles-of-service-design-thinking-building-better-services

Von Saldern, M. (1992): Qualitative Forschung - Quantitative Forschung. Nekrolog auf einen Gegensatz, in: Empirische Paedagogik, vol. 6 (editor) (1992), pp. 377-399

Wacker, S. (2018): Customer Experience: Das kuenftige Schlachtfeld des Wettbewerbs. Wettbewerbsfaktor Kundenerlebnis – Service Design setzt genau hier an. Retrieved November 20, 2018 from https://www.der-bank-blog.de/kundenerlebnis-wettbewerbsvorteil/customer-experience/33358/

Walters, J. (n.d.): What is a customer touchpoint? Retrieved September 30, 2018 from http://360connext.com/customer-touchpoint/

Weiß, M. (2018): Vom Kundenservice-Center zum Omnikanal-Center (Kunden-Dialog-Center). Retrieved November 22, 2018 from https://www.banken-undpartner.de/nachricht/vom-kundenservice-center-zum-omnikanal-center-kundendialog-center/

Wolf, B. / Priebe, M. (2003): Wissenschaftstheoretische Richtungen. Forschung, Statistik & Methoden. Verlag Empirische Paedagogik, Landau in der Pfalz

Wolf, S. (2008): Der Methodenstreit quantitativer und qualitativer Sozialforschung unter besonderer Beruecksichtigung der grundlegenden Unterschiede beider Forschungstraditionen. Retrieved November 18, 2018 from http://websquare.imb-uni-augsburg.de/files/Bachelorarbeit_Wolf.pdf

List of Appendices

Appendix 1: Customer interview 1

Researcher: Christopher Rossmann

Name	Customer 1 (Anonymized)
Age and gender	32, male
Profession / current job	Logistician
Industry	Public service
Date and length of interview	November 9, 2018, 60 minutes
Type of interview	Personal interview
Language of interview	German. Questions are translated to English. Responses are not translated. Significant responses and parts of the interview are used to create a customer journey map in the thesis.
Quality and content check	The created customer journey map was sent to the participant afterwards for validation.

Gliederung des Interviews. Structure of the interview140

A) Narrativer Teil. Narrative part.

B) Emotionszentrierter Teil. Emotion-based part.

A)* Narrativer Teil. *Narrative part.

1. Einführung in das Thema, Rahmen und Zielsetzung der Arbeit. Introduction, *Frame and objective of the work.*

2. Information zum Interviewablauf und zur Dauer. *Information about the interview structure and length.*

3. Datenschutzvereinbarung: Anonymisierte Verwendung der Kundendaten nur mit Alter, Beruf, Branche. *Data protection agreement: using customer data anonymized: age, profession and industry.*

4. Seit wann sind Sie Kunde der Sparkasse? *How long have you been customer of the savings bank?*

- *For more than 5 years.*

5. Welche Produkte der Sparkasse nutzen Sie? *Which products, services and subscriptions of the savings banks are you using currently?*

---

140 cf. Oberholzer/Eichholzer (2017), p. 21

- *Checking account, credit card, securities account, Travel health insurance, mortgage loan, building society contract.*

6. Wann war Ihr letztes ganzheitliches Beratungsgespräch? *When have you had your last comprehensive consultation?*

- *Summer 2017*

7. Mit welchen Anlässen sind Sie zuletzt auf die Berater der Sparkasse zugegangen? *For which reasons did you recently contact the advisors of the savings bank?*

- *Inheritance and contract transfers.*
- *Consultation on applying for a mortgage loan*

8. Mit welchen Anlässen wurden Sie zuletzt zu einem Beratungsgespräch seitens der Sparkasse eingeladen? *For which reasons were you recently contacted by the savings bank to schedule an appointment for a consultation?*

- *There have not been any calls or attempts to schedule an appointment.*

B) Emotionszentrierter Teil. *Emotion-based part.*

Bewertung und Beschreibung der Kontaktpunkte durch den Kunden nach Pain- und Pleasure Points, Emotionen und den Gründen für das Empfinden des Kunden. Nach Möglichkeit: strukturierte Abfolge der Ereignisse. *Evaluation and explanation of the touch points by the customer considering pain and pleasure points and emotions. Asking for the reasons of the customer's feelings. If possible: structured sequence of the events.* Antworten sind dargestellt in der Customer Journey map. *Responses are illustrated in the customer journey map.*

Eine Auswahl der gestellten Fragen während der Interviews. *A selection of questions used during the interviews:*

- Welche Kanäle haben Sie genutzt und warum? *Which channels did you use and why?*
- Wie haben Sie die Kanäle wahrgenommen? *How did you perceive the channels?*
- Wie haben Sie sich gefühlt in dieser Phase des Prozesses und was dachten Sie dabei? *How did you feel during that stage of the journey and what did you think?*
- Was waren die Auslöser für diese Entscheidung? *What was the trigger for you to make that decision?*

- War das eine positive, negative oder neutrale Erfahrung in Bezug zu Ihren Erwartungen? *Was that a positive, negative or neutral experience in regard to your expectations?*
- Können Sie Ihr Gefühl in einem einzigen Wort ausdrücken? *Can you express your feeling by using a single word?*
- Welche Maßnahmen der Bank haben Ihre Erwartungen übertroffen, erfüllt und nicht erfüllt? *Which actions by the bank did surpass, meet and not meet your expectations?*
- Welche Kontaktpunkte und Maßnahmen der Bank waren enttäuschend oder verbesserungswürdig nach Ihrer Meinung? *Which touchpoints and actions by the bank were disappointing or improvable in your opinion and why?*
- Welche Hürden sind aufgetreten? *Which obstacles did you face?*
- Welche Medien hat der Berater während der Beratung genutzt und wie haben Ihnen diese gefallen? *Which media did the advisor use during the consultation and how did you like them?*

Appendix 2: Customer interview 2

Researcher: Christopher Rossmann

Name	Customer 2 (Anonymized)
Age and gender	25, male
Profession / current job	Electronics mechanic
Industry	Metal and electro
Date and length of interview	November 10, 2018, 55 minutes
Type of interview	Telephone interview
Language of interview	German. Questions are translated to English. Responses are not translated. Significant responses and parts of the interview are used to create a customer journey map in the thesis.
Quality and content check	The created customer journey map was sent to the participant afterwards for validation.

Gliederung des Interviews. Structure of the interview141

A) Narrativer Teil. *Narrative part.*

B) Emotionszentrierter Teil. *Emotion-based part.*

A) Narrativer Teil. *Narrative part.*

1. Einführung in das Thema, Rahmen und Zielsetzung der Arbeit. *Introduction, Frame and objective of the work.*

2. Information zum Interviewablauf und zur Dauer. *Information about the interview structure and length.*

3. Datenschutzvereinbarung: Anonymisierte Verwendung der Kundendaten nur mit Alter, Beruf, Branche. *Data protection agreement: using customer data anonymized: age, profession and industry.*

4. Seit wann sind Sie Kunde der Sparkasse? *How long have you been customer of the savings bank?*

- *For more than 10 years.*

[141] cf. Oberholzer/Eichholzer (2017), p. 21

5. Welche Produkte der Sparkasse nutzen Sie? *Which products, services and subscriptions of the savings banks are you using currently?*

- *Checking account, credit card, building society contract, pension savings plan, investment fund savings plan, securities account, several savings accounts.*

6. Wann war Ihr letztes ganzheitliches Beratungsgespräch? *When have you had your last comprehensive consultation?*

- *April 2018*

7. Mit welchen Anlässen sind Sie zuletzt auf die Berater der Sparkasse zugegangen? *For which reasons did you recently contact the advisors of the savings bank?*

- *Completing a travel health insurance*
- *Comparing insurances in customer's portfolio with a settlement offer by a competitor.*

8. Mit welchen Anlässen wurden Sie zuletzt zu einem Beratungsgespräch seitens der Sparkasse eingeladen? *For which reasons were you recently contacted by the savings bank to schedule an appointment for a consultation?*

- *Scheduling a comprehensive bank consultation ("Finanzcheck") to check customer's portfolio of financial products.*

B) Emotionszentrierter Teil. *Emotion-based part.*

Bewertung und Beschreibung der Kontaktpunkte durch den Kunden nach Pain- und Pleasure Points, Emotionen und den Gründen für das Empfinden des Kunden. Nach Möglichkeit: strukturierte Abfolge der Ereignisse. *Evaluation and explanation of the touch points by the customer considering pain and pleasure points and emotions. Asking for the reasons of the customer's feelings. If possible: structured sequence of the events.* Antworten sind dargestellt in der Customer Journey map. *Responses are illustrated in the customer journey map.*

Eine Auswahl der gestellten Fragen während der Interviews. *A selection of questions used during the interviews:*

- Welche Kanäle haben Sie genutzt und warum? *Which channels did you use and why?*
- Wie haben Sie die Kanäle wahrgenommen? *How did you perceive the channels?*
- Wie haben Sie sich gefühlt in dieser Phase des Prozesses und was dachten Sie dabei? *How did you feel during that stage of the journey and what did you think?*

- Was waren die Auslöser für diese Entscheidung? *What was the trigger for you to make that decision?*
- War das eine positive, negative oder neutrale Erfahrung in Bezug zu Ihren Erwartungen? *Was that a positive, negative or neutral experience in regard to your expectations?*
- Können Sie Ihr Gefühl in einem einzigen Wort ausdrücken? *Can you express your feeling by using a single word?*
- Welche Maßnahmen der Bank haben Ihre Erwartungen übertroffen, erfüllt und nicht erfüllt? *Which actions by the bank did surpass, meet and not meet your expectations?*
- Welche Kontaktpunkte und Maßnahmen der Bank waren enttäuschend oder verbesserungswürdig nach Ihrer Meinung? *Which touchpoints and actions by the bank were disappointing or improvable in your opinion and why?*
- Welche Hürden sind aufgetreten? *Which obstacles did you face?*
- Welche Medien hat der Berater während der Beratung genutzt und wie haben Ihnen diese gefallen? *Which media did the advisor use during the consultation and how did you like them?*

Appendix 3: Customer interview 3

Researcher: Christopher Rossmann

Name	Customer 3 (Anonymized)
Age and gender	25, female
Profession / current job	Student
Industry	Student
Date and length of interview	November 12, 2018, 40 minutes
Type of interview	Personal interview
Language of interview	German. Questions and responds are translated to English. Significant responses and parts of the interview are used to create a customer journey map in the thesis.
Quality and content check	The created customer journey map was sent to the participant afterwards for validation.

Gliederung des Interviews. *Structure of the interview*[142]

A) Narrativer Teil. *Narrative part.*

B) Emotionszentrierter Teil. *Emotion-based part.*

A) Narrativer Teil. *Narrative part.*

1. Einführung in das Thema, Rahmen und Zielsetzung der Arbeit. *Introduction, Frame and objective of the work.*

2. Information zum Interviewablauf und zur Dauer. *Information about the interview structure and length.*

3. Datenschutzvereinbarung: Anonymisierte Verwendung der Kundendaten nur mit Alter, Beruf, Branche. *Data protection agreement: using customer data anonymized: age, profession and industry.*

4. Seit wann sind Sie Kunde der Sparkasse? *How long have you been customer of the savings bank?*

- *For more than 9 years.*

[142] cf. Oberholzer/Eichholzer (2017), p. 21

5. Welche Produkte der Sparkasse nutzen Sie? *Which products, services and subscriptions of the savings banks are you using currently?*

- *Checking account.*

6. Wann war Ihr letztes ganzheitliches Beratungsgespräch? *When have you had your last comprehensive consultation?*

- *December 2017.*

7. Mit welchen Anlässen sind Sie zuletzt auf die Berater der Sparkasse zugegangen? *For which reasons did you recently contact the advisors of the savings bank?*

- *-/-*

8. Mit welchen Anlässen wurden Sie zuletzt zu einem Beratungsgespräch seitens der Sparkasse eingeladen? *For which reasons were you recently contacted by the savings bank to schedule an appointment for a consultation?*

- *Update of lodged sample signature utilized to authorize transactions.*

B) Emotionszentrierter Teil. *Emotion-based part.*

Bewertung und Beschreibung der Kontaktpunkte durch den Kunden nach Pain- und Pleasure Points, Emotionen und den Gründen für das Empfinden des Kunden. Nach Möglichkeit: strukturierte Abfolge der Ereignisse. *Evaluation and explanation of the touch points by the customer considering pain and pleasure points and emotions. Asking for the reasons of the customer's feelings. If possible: structured sequence of the events.* Antworten sind dargestellt in der Customer Journey map. *Responses are illustrated in the customer journey map.*

Eine Auswahl der gestellten Fragen während der Interviews. *A selection of questions used during the interviews:*

- Welche Kanäle haben Sie genutzt und warum? *Which channels did you use and why?*
- Wie haben Sie die Kanäle wahrgenommen? *How did you perceive the channels?*
- Wie haben Sie sich gefühlt in dieser Phase des Prozesses und was dachten Sie dabei? *How did you feel during that stage of the journey and what did you think?*
- Was waren die Auslöser für diese Entscheidung? *What was the trigger for you to make that decision?*

- War das eine positive, negative oder neutrale Erfahrung in Bezug zu Ihren Erwartungen? *Was that a positive, negative or neutral experience in regard to your expectations?*
- Können Sie Ihr Gefühl in einem einzigen Wort ausdrücken? *Can you express your feeling by using a single word?*
- Welche Maßnahmen der Bank haben Ihre Erwartungen übertroffen, erfüllt und nicht erfüllt? *Which actions by the bank did surpass, meet and not meet your expectations?*
- Welche Kontaktpunkte und Maßnahmen der Bank waren enttäuschend oder verbesserungswürdig nach Ihrer Meinung? *Which touchpoints and actions by the bank were disappointing or improvable in your opinion and why?*
- Welche Hürden sind aufgetreten? *Which obstacles did you face?*
- Welche Medien hat der Berater während der Beratung genutzt und wie haben Ihnen diese gefallen? *Which media did the advisor use during the consultation and how did you like them?*

Appendix 4: Customer interview 4

Researcher: Christopher Rossmann

Name	Customer 4 (Anonymized)
Primary financial institution	Sparkasse Y (Anonymzed)[143]
Age and gender	35, male
Profession / current job	Legal assistant
Industry	Law
Date and length of interview	November 14, 2018, 55 minutes
Type of interview	Personal interview
Language of interview	German. Questions are translated to English. Responses are not translated. Significant responses and parts of the interview are used to create a customer journey map in the thesis.
Quality and content check	The created customer journey map was sent to the participant afterwards for validation.

Gliederung des Interviews. *Structure of the interview*[144]

A) Narrativer Teil. *Narrative part.*

B) Emotionszentrierter Teil. *Emotion-based part.*

A) Narrativer Teil. *Narrative part.*

1. Einführung in das Thema, Rahmen und Zielsetzung der Arbeit. *Introduction, Frame and objective of the work.*

2. Information zum Interviewablauf und zur Dauer. *Information about the interview structure and length.*

3. Datenschutzvereinbarung: Anonymisierte Verwendung der Kundendaten nur mit Alter, Beruf, Branche. *Data protection agreement: using customer data anonymized: age, profession and industry.*

143 The primary financial institution differs from the sample bank. This savings bank differs not significantly in strategic direction as well as size of the sample bank.

144 cf. Oberholzer/Eichholzer (2017), p. 21

4. Seit wann sind Sie Kunde der Sparkasse? *How long have you been customer of the savings bank?*

- *For more than 15 years.*

5. Welche Produkte der Sparkasse nutzen Sie? *Which products, services and subscriptions of the savings banks are you using currently?*

- *Checking account, credit card, investment fund pension plan, investment fund savings plan, building society contract.*

6. Wann war Ihr letztes ganzheitliches Beratungsgespräch? *When have you had your last comprehensive consultation?*

- *October 2018*

7. Mit welchen Anlässen sind Sie zuletzt auf die Berater der Sparkasse zugegangen? *For which reasons did you recently contact the advisors of the savings bank?*

- *Opening a savings plan for new born son.*
- *Customer received letter which stated credit card got was blocked as a precaution due to fraud prevention.*

8. Mit welchen Anlässen wurden Sie zuletzt zu einem Beratungsgespräch seitens der Sparkasse eingeladen? *For which reasons were you recently contacted by the savings bank to schedule an appointment for a consultation?*

- *Known personal advisor called and scheduled appointment because of the due date of a building society contract in customer's portfolio.*

B) Emotionszentrierter Teil. *Emotion-based part.*

Bewertung und Beschreibung der Kontaktpunkte durch den Kunden nach Pain- und Pleasure Points, Emotionen und den Gründen für das Empfinden des Kunden. Nach Möglichkeit: strukturierte Abfolge der Ereignisse. *Evaluation and explanation of the touch points by the customer considering pain and pleasure points and emotions. Asking for the reasons of the customer's feelings. If possible: structured sequence of the events.* Antworten sind dargestellt in der Customer Journey map. *Responses are illustrated in the customer journey map.*

Eine Auswahl der gestellten Fragen während der Interviews. *A selection of questions used during the interviews:*

- Welche Kanäle haben Sie genutzt und warum? *Which channels did you use and why?*

- Wie haben Sie die Kanäle wahrgenommen? *How did you perceive the channels?*
- Wie haben Sie sich gefühlt in dieser Phase des Prozesses und was dachten Sie dabei? *How did you feel during that stage of the journey and what did you think?*
- Was waren die Auslöser für diese Entscheidung? *What was the trigger for you to make that decision?*
- War das eine positive, negative oder neutrale Erfahrung in Bezug zu Ihren Erwartungen? *Was that a positive, negative or neutral experience in regard to your expectations?*
- Können Sie Ihr Gefühl in einem einzigen Wort ausdrücken? *Can you express your feeling by using a single word?*
- Welche Maßnahmen der Bank haben Ihre Erwartungen übertroffen, erfüllt und nicht erfüllt? *Which actions by the bank did surpass, meet and not meet your expectations?*
- Welche Kontaktpunkte und Maßnahmen der Bank waren enttäuschend oder verbesserungswürdig nach Ihrer Meinung? *Which touchpoints and actions by the bank were disappointing or improvable in your opinion and why?*
- Welche Hürden sind aufgetreten? *Which obstacles did you face?*
- Welche Medien hat der Berater während der Beratung genutzt und wie haben Ihnen diese gefallen? *Which media did the advisor use during the consultation and how did you like them?*

Appendix 5: Customer interview 5

Researcher: Christopher Rossmann

Name	Customer 5 (Anonymized)
Primary financial institution	Sparkasse X (Anonymized)
Age and gender	35, male
Profession / current job	Human resources accountant
Industry	Metal processing
Date and length of interview	November 20, 2018, 65 minutes
Type of interview	Personal interview
Language of interview	German. Questions are translated to English. Responses are not translated. Significant responses and parts of the interview are used to create a customer journey map in the thesis.
Quality and content check	The created customer journey map was sent to the participant afterwards for validation.

Gliederung des Interviews. *Structure of the interview*[145]

A) Narrativer Teil. *Narrative part.*

B) Emotionszentrierter Teil. *Emotion-based part.*

A) Narrativer Teil. *Narrative part.*

1. Einführung in das Thema, Rahmen und Zielsetzung der Arbeit. *Introduction, Frame and objective of the work.*

2. Information zum Interviewablauf und zur Dauer. *Information about the interview structure and length.*

3. Datenschutzvereinbarung: Anonymisierte Verwendung der Kundendaten nur mit Alter, Beruf, Branche. *Data protection agreement: using customer data anonymized: age, profession and industry.*

4. Seit wann sind Sie Kunde der Sparkasse? *How long have you been customer of the savings bank?*

- *For more than 10 years.*

[145] cf. Oberholzer/Eichholzer (2017), p. 21

5. Welche Produkte der Sparkasse nutzen Sie? *Which products, services and subscriptions of the savings banks are you using currently?*

- *Checking account, credit card, building society contract, securities account, third-liability insurance, legal insurance, pension insurance*

6. Wann war Ihr letztes ganzheitliches Beratungsgespräch? *When have you had your last comprehensive consultation?*

- *March 2018*

7. Mit welchen Anlässen sind Sie zuletzt auf die Berater der Sparkasse zugegangen? *For which reasons did you recently contact the advicers of the savings bank?*

- Car loan because of intended car purchase
- Opening a savings plan for new born son.
- Advice on a mortgage loan for prospective investment in real estate.
- Change internet banking limit for making a transaction (phone call).

8. Mit welchen Anlässen wurden Sie zuletzt zu einem Beratungsgespräch seitens der Sparkasse eingeladen? *For which reasons were you recently contacted by the savings bank to schedule an appointment for a consultation?*

- Using state supported products.

B) Emotionszentrierter Teil. *Emotion-based part.*

Bewertung und Beschreibung der Kontaktpunkte durch den Kunden nach Pain- und Pleasure Points, Emotionen und den Gründen für das Empfinden des Kunden. Nach Möglichkeit: strukturierte Abfolge der Ereignisse. *Evaluation and explanation of the touch points by the customer considering pain and pleasure points and emotions. Asking for the reasons of the customer's feelings. If possible: structured sequence of the events.* Antworten sind dargestellt in der Customer Journey map. *Responses are illustrated in the customer journey map.*

Eine Auswahl der gestellten Fragen während der Interviews. *A selection of questions used during the interviews:*

- Welche Kanäle haben Sie genutzt und warum? *Which channels did you use and why?*
- Wie haben Sie die Kanäle wahrgenommen? *How did you perceive the channels?*
- Wie haben Sie sich gefühlt in dieser Phase des Prozesses und was dachten Sie dabei? *How did you feel during that stage of the journey and what did you think?*

- Was waren die Auslöser für diese Entscheidung? *What was the trigger for you to make that decision?*
- War das eine positive, negative oder neutrale Erfahrung in Bezug zu Ihren Erwartungen? *Was that a positive, negative or neutral experience in regard to your expectations?*
- Können Sie Ihr Gefühl in einem einzigen Wort ausdrücken? *Can you express your feeling by using a single word?*
- Welche Maßnahmen der Bank haben Ihre Erwartungen übertroffen, erfüllt und nicht erfüllt? *Which actions by the bank did surpass, meet and not meet your expectations?*
- Welche Kontaktpunkte und Maßnahmen der Bank waren enttäuschend oder verbesserungswürdig nach Ihrer Meinung? *Which touchpoints and actions by the bank were disappointing or improvable in your opinion and why?*
- Welche Hürden sind aufgetreten? *Which obstacles did you face?*
- Welche Medien hat der Berater während der Beratung genutzt und wie haben Ihnen diese gefallen? *Which media did the advisor use during the consultation and how did you like them?*

Appendix 6: Customer interview 6

Researcher: Christopher Rossmann

Name	Customer 6 (Anonymized)
Primary financial institution	Sparkasse Z (Anonymzed)[146]
Age and gender	33, male
Profession / current job	Software engineer
Industry	IT
Date and length of interview	November 23, 2018, 50 minutes
Type of interview	Personal interview
Language of interview	German. Questions are translated to English. Responses are not translated. Significant responses and parts of the interview are used to create a customer journey map in the thesis.
Quality and content check	The created customer journey map was sent to the participant afterwards for validation.

Gliederung des Interviews. *Structure of the interview*[147]

A) Narrativer Teil. *Narrative part.*

B) Emotionszentrierter Teil. *Emotion-based part.*

A) Narrativer Teil. *Narrative part.*

2. Einführung in das Thema, Rahmen und Zielsetzung der Arbeit. *Introduction, Frame and objective of the work.*

3. Information zum Interviewablauf und zur Dauer. *Information about the interview structure and length.*

4. Datenschutzvereinbarung: Anonymisierte Verwendung der Kundendaten nur mit Alter, Beruf, Branche. *Data protection agreement: using customer data anonymized: age, profession and industry.*

[146] The primary financial institution differs from the sample bank. This savings bank differs not significantly in strategic direction as well as size of the sample bank.

[147] cf. Oberholzer/Eichholzer (2017), p. 21

5. Seit wann sind Sie Kunde der Sparkasse? *How long have you been customer of the savings bank?*

- *For more than 20 years.*

6. Welche Produkte der Sparkasse nutzen Sie? *Which products, services and subscriptions of the savings banks are you using currently?*

- *Checking account, mortgage loan, building society contract, real estate insurance*

7. Wann war Ihr letztes ganzheitliches Beratungsgespräch? *When have you had your last comprehensive consultation?*

- *Never*

8. Mit welchen Anlässen sind Sie zuletzt auf die Berater der Sparkasse zugegangen? *For which reasons did you recently contact the advisors of the savings bank?*

- *Pre-termination agreement of mortgage loan in customer's portfolio*
- *Overdraft facility*

9. Mit welchen Anlässen wurden Sie zuletzt zu einem Beratungsgespräch seitens der Sparkasse eingeladen? *For which reasons were you recently contacted by the savings bank to schedule an appointment for a consultation?*

- Pension insurance

B) Emotionszentrierter Teil. *Emotion-based part.*

Bewertung und Beschreibung der Kontaktpunkte durch den Kunden nach Pain- und Pleasure Points, Emotionen und den Gründen für das Empfinden des Kunden. Nach Möglichkeit: strukturierte Abfolge der Ereignisse. *Evaluation and explanation of the touch points by the customer considering pain and pleasure points and emotions. Asking for the reasons of the customer's feelings. If possible: structured sequence of the events.* Antworten sind dargestellt in der Customer Journey map. *Responses are illustrated in the customer journey map.*

Eine Auswahl der gestellten Fragen während der Interviews. *A selection of questions used during the interviews:*

- Welche Kanäle haben Sie genutzt und warum? *Which channels did you use and why?*

- Wie haben Sie die Kanäle wahrgenommen? *How did you perceive the channels?*
- Wie haben Sie sich gefühlt in dieser Phase des Prozesses und was dachten Sie dabei? *How did you feel during that stage of the journey and what did you think?*
- Was waren die Auslöser für diese Entscheidung? *What was the trigger for you to make that decision?*
- War das eine positive, negative oder neutrale Erfahrung in Bezug zu Ihren Erwartungen? *Was that a positive, negative or neutral experience in regard to your expectations?*
- Können Sie Ihr Gefühl in einem einzigen Wort ausdrücken? *Can you express your feeling by using a single word?*
- Welche Maßnahmen der Bank haben Ihre Erwartungen übertroffen, erfüllt und nicht erfüllt? *Which actions by the bank did surpass, meet and not meet your expectations?*
- Welche Kontaktpunkte und Maßnahmen der Bank waren enttäuschend oder verbesserungswürdig nach Ihrer Meinung? *Which touchpoints and actions by the bank were disappointing or improvable in your opinion and why?*
- Welche Hürden sind aufgetreten? *Which obstacles did you face?*
- Welche Medien hat der Berater während der Beratung genutzt und wie haben Ihnen diese gefallen? *Which media did the advisor use during the consultation and how did you like them?*

Appendix 7: Expert interview Sparkasse 1

Researcher: Christopher Rossmann

Name and age of interviewe partner	Expert 1 (Anonymized)
Company/Organization	Sparkasse 1 (Anonymzed) (savings bank)
Position/Job and term	Head of unit: sales branches Since 2016
Professional career	Former positions as sales director and branch manager within the same organization.
Date and time of interview	November 7, 2018, 09.00-10:45 am.
Location of interview	Headquarters of Sparkasse 1
Language of interview	German. Questions are translated to English. Responses are not translated. Significant responses and parts of the interview are used as quotations and paraphrases in the thesis.
Quality and content check	This interview script was sent afterwards to the interviewee for validation.

Interview zur Anwendung und Wahrnehmung des Sparkassen-Finanzkonzepts aus der Sichtweise von Vertriebsmitarbeitern. Interview about the application and perception of the comprehensive bank consultation approach with the point of view of sales representatives.

Interviewziele: Lösung der Forschungsfrage unterstützen, Problemfelder aufzeigen, Erkenntnisse für Verbesserungsvorschläge gewinnen.

Interview goals: assist in replying to the research question, uncover issues, gain insight to make improvement proposals.

Gliederung des Interviews. Structure of the interview Offene Fragen. Open questions Antworten in Stichpunkten. Responses in bullet points.

1. Einführung in das Thema, Rahmen und Zielsetzung der Arbeit. *Introduction, Frame and objective of the work.*

2. Information zum Interviewablauf und zur Dauer. *Information about the interview structure and length.*

3. Datenschutzvereinbarung: Nennung von Name, Funktion in der Bank, kurzer Werdegang und Alter. *Data protection agreement: Name, position in the bank, brief describtion of professional career and age will be mentioned.*

4. *Wie wichtig ist das Girokonto des Kunden als Basis für den Absatz weiterer Produkte bei Sparkassen? How important is the checking account of a customer as a basis for selling additional products at savings banks?*

- *Response removed due to data protection policy.*

5. *Wie beurteilen Sie die Fähigkeit und Kompetenz der Vertriebsmitarbeiter von Sparkassen zum Absatz von Produkten bei a) Nichtkunden und b) Kunden mit ihrem Hauptgirokonto bei einem Mitbewerber? How do you evaluate the capability and expertise of the savings bank's sales representatives regarding selling products to a) non-customers and b) customers holding their primary checking account at a competitor?*

- *a) Nichtkunden:*
- *Response removed due to data protection policy.*
- *b) Kunden mit Hauptgirokonto bei einem Mitbewerber*
- *Response removed due to data protection policy.*

6. *Wie erfolgt die Vereinbarung von ganzheitlichen Beratungsgesprächen im Sparkassenvertrieb am erfolgversprechendsten? What is the most successful way to schedule comprehensive consultations by sales representatives of the savings banks?*

- *Response removed due to data protection policy.*

7. Durch welche Prozesse werden Sparkassen-Finanzkonzeptgespräche bei der Sparkasse 1 vereinbart? Through which processes are comprehensive bank consultations scheduled at Sparkasse 1?

- *Response removed due to data protection policy.*

8. *Gibt es einen Leitfaden oder eine Struktur für die Vertriebsmitarbeiter für die Anwendung des Sparkassen-Finanzkonzepts? Are there guidelines or is there a structure for the sales representatives regarding the application of the comprehensive bank consultations?*

- *Response removed due to data protection policy.*

9. Wo liegen die Stärken und Schwächen des Sparkassen-Finanzkonzepts? Bei separater Betrachtung in der Wahrnehmung von Vertriebsmitarbeitern und Kunden. *What are the strengths and weaknesses of comprehensive bank consultations of the German savings banks? If you consider the perception of sales representatives and customers separately.*

- Pro:
- *Response removed due to data protection policy.*
- Contra:
- *Response removed due to data protection policy.*

10. Sonstiges / *Other comments:*

- *Response removed due to data protection policy.*

Appendix 8: Expert interview Sparkasse 2

Researcher: Christopher Rossmann

Name and age of interview partner	Expert 2 (Anonymized)
Company/Organization	Sparkasse 2 (Anonymized) (savings bank)
Position/Job and term	Specialist for XXX in department sales distribution. Project member securities and investment products customer journey.
Professional career	XXX
Educational background	Bachelor of Science in Finance
Date and time of interview	December, 1, 2018, 11:30 - 1:25 pm.
Location of interview	Telephone interview
Language of interview	German. Questions and responses are not translated. Significant responses and parts of the interview are summarized and evaluated in the thesis.
Quality and content check	This interview script was sent afterwards to the interviewee for validation.

Interview zu den Erfahrungen aus der Durchführung eines CJA-Projekts in einer großen Sparkasse. Interview about the experiences with an actually conducted CJA project in a large savings bank in Germany.

Interviewziele: Lösung der Forschungsfrage unterstützen, Abgleich mit theoretischen Erkenntnissen und diese gegebenenfalls ergänzen.

Interview goals: assist in replying to research question as well as matching and optionally completing the theoretical findings.

Gliederung des Interviews. Structure of the interview Strukturiertes Interview. Ausgewählte Fragen anhand des Bearbeitungsstands des theoretischen und praktischen Teils der Arbeit zum Zeitpunkt des Interviews. *Structured interview. Questions were selected on behalf of the status of the theoretical and empirical part of the papier on the date of the interview.*

Übersicht / At a glance

A) Einführung. Introduction

B) Inhaltlicher Teil. Content-related part.

A. Einführung. *Introduction*

11. Einführung in das Thema, Rahmen und Zielsetzung der Arbeit. Introduction, Frame and objective of the work.

12. Information zum Interviewablauf und zur Dauer. *Information about the interview structure and length.*

13. Datenschutzvereinbarung: Nennung von Name, Funktion in der Bank, kurzer Werdegang und Alter. *Data protection agreement: Name, position in the bank, brief description of professional career, educational background and age will be mentioned.*

B. Inhaltlicher Teil. *Content-related part.*

1. In welcher Art wurde die Customer Journey Analyse als Projekt initiiert?

Response removed due to data protection policy.

2. Wer war Auftraggeber des Projekts und wie wurden Änderungsvorschläge als Ergebnis aus dem Projekt implementiert?

Response removed due to data protection policy.

3. Wie wurde das Projektmanagement gestaltet?

Response removed due to data protection policy.

4. Was sind die Projektziele?

Response removed due to data protection policy.

5. Gab es konkrete Businessprobleme, die gelöst werden sollten?

Response removed due to data protection policy.

6. Gab es Key Performance Indicators (KPI), die gemessen und verbessert werden sollten?

Response removed due to data protection policy.

7. Wie viele Mitarbeiter sind am Projekt beteiligt?

Response removed due to data protection policy.

8. Wie viele Mitarbeiter sind konkret an der Customer Journey Analyse beteiligt und wie erfolgte das Mapping?

Response removed due to data protection policy.

9. Welche Kundenzielgruppe wurden betrachtet?

Response removed due to data protection policy.

10. Wie gestaltet sich die Meilenstein- und Zeitplanung des Projekts?

Response removed due to data protection policy.

11. Mit welcher Methode wurden Daten für die Customer Journey erhoben?

Response removed due to data protection policy.

12. Wie wurden die Interviews hinsichtlich Akquisition und Entlohnung der Kunden gestaltet?

Response removed due to data protection policy.

13. Wie lange dauerten die Interviews und wie waren sie strukturiert?

Response removed due to data protection policy.

14. Wurde sich auf einen bestimmten Teil der Kundenreise konzentriert?

Response removed due to data protection policy.

15. Was waren identifizierte Pain und Pleasure Points als Erkenntnisse aus der Customer Journey?

Pain Points:

Response removed due to data protection policy.

Pleasure Points:

Response removed due to data protection policy.

16. Gab es weitere besondere Kernerkenntnisse hinsichtlich der Kundenzielgruppen?

Response removed due to data protection policy.

17. Welche Kernerkenntnisse gibt es aus den geführten Mitarbeiterinterviews?

Response removed due to data protection policy.

18. Welche konkreten Umsetzungsempfehlungen gibt es bislang aus dem Projekt und was soll damit erreicht werden (insbesondere KPIs)?

Response removed due to data protection policy.

Beratung und Prozessmanagement:

Response removed due to data protection policy.

19. Wie bewerten Sie die Sinnhaftigkeit einer Customer Journey Analyse in Sparkassen basierend auf den Erfahrungen aus diesem Projekt?

Response removed due to data protection policy.

20. Gab es schon mal ähnliche Projekte in der Sparkasse?

Response removed due to data protection policy.

21. Was sind die weiteren Schritte?

Response removed due to data protection policy.